Grammar Sense 1B

SECOND EDITION

SERIES DIRECTOR
Susan Kesner Bland

AUTHOR
Cheryl Pavlik

OXFORD
UNIVERSITY PRESS

OXFORD
UNIVERSITY PRESS

198 Madison Avenue
New York, NY 10016 USA

Great Clarendon Street, Oxford, OX2 6DP, United Kingdom

Oxford University Press is a department of the University of Oxford.
It furthers the University's objective of excellence in research, scholarship,
and education by publishing worldwide. Oxford is a registered trade
mark of Oxford University Press in the UK and in certain other countries

General Manager, American ELT: Laura Pearson
Publisher: Stephanie Karras
Associate Publishing Manager: Sharon Sargent
Managing Editor: Alex Ragan
Director, ADP: Susan Sanguily
Executive Design Manager: Maj-Britt Hagsted
Electronic Production Manager: Julie Armstrong
Senior Designer: Yin Ling Wong
Image Manager: Trisha Masterson

Publishing and Editorial Management: hyphen S.A.

ISBN: 978 0 19 448912 6 Student Book 1B with Online Practice pack
ISBN: 978 0 19 448902 7 Student Book 1B as pack component
ISBN: 978 0 19 448928 7 Online Practice as pack component

Printed in China

This book is printed on paper from certified and well-managed sources

ACKNOWLEDGEMENTS

Illustrations by: Thanos Tsilis (hyphen): 4, 5, 6, 10, 11, 38, 52, 53, 54, 110,
121, 148, 161, 171, 194, 253, 302, 328; Alexandros Tzimeros / SmartMagna
(hyphen): 16, 28, 35, 44, 45, 48, 78, 82, 188, 196, 199, 257, 258, 271, 285;
Bart Bastian: 248

*We would also like to thank the following for permission to reproduce the following
photographs*: Devation - Edwin Verbruggen / www.shutterstock.com,
Andreas Gradin / www.shutterstock.com, homydesign /
www.shutterstock.com, marekuliasz / www.shutterstock.com, Travel Ink /
Getty Images, Cover l to r and interior; Marcin Krygier / iStockphoto, Front
matter and back cover (laptop); OUP / OUPpicturebank, pg. 3 (pencil); D.
Hurst / OUPpicturebank, pg. 3 (computer); Wallenrock / Shutterstock,
pg. 3 (computers); D. Hurst / OUPpicturebank, pg. 3 (book); Photodisc
/ OUPpicturebank, pg. 3 (books); Baloncici / Shutterstock, pg. 3 (desk);
vovan / Shutterstock, pg. 3 (calendar); HomeStudio / Shutterstock,
pg. 3 (calendars); Yuri Arcurs / Shutterstock, pg. 3 (student); Kurhan
/ Shutterstock, pg. 3 (students); Colour / Shutterstock, pg. 23 (man);
Photodisc / OUPpicturebank, pg. 23 (flowers); Photodisc / OUPpicturebank,
pg. 23 (elephant); Photodisc / OUPpicturebank, pg. 23 (ladybug); Photodisc
/ OUPpicturebank, pg. 23 (spider); Photodisc / OUPpicturebank, pg. 23
(toddler); wavebreakmedia ltd / Shutterstock, pg. 24; Gareth Boden /
OUPpicturebank, pg. 31; Adams Picture Library / OUPpicturebank, pg.
60 (apartment building); Chee-Onn Leong / Shutterstock, pg. 60 (brick
building); Philipus / OUPpicturebank, pg. 60 (house); Mike McDonald
/ Shutterstock, pg. 75; OUP / OUPpicturebank, pg. 88; Barry Blackburn
/ Shutterstock, pg. 89; Tim Pannell / Corbis, pg. 94; WhitePlaid /
Shutterstock, pg. 96 (cat); Comstock / OUPpicturebank, pg. 96 (sofa);
White / OUPpicturebank, pg. 96 (table); White / OUPpicturebank, pg. 96
(chair); Photodisc / OUPpicturebank, pg. 100; Photodisc / OUPpicturebank,
pg. 101; Photodisc / OUPpicturebank, pg. 109; Kletr / Shutterstock, pg.
114 (plants); OUP / OUPpicturebank, pg. 114 (glasses); Antoha713 /
Shutterstock, pg. 114 (window); Darby Sawchuk / OUPpicturebank, pg.
114 (clock); Bill Grove / istockphoto, pg. 114 (school); Brand X Pictures /
OUPpicturebank, pg. 114 (books); PhotoAlto / OUPpicturebank, pg. 128
(reading newspaper); Polka Dot Images / OUPpicturebank, pg. 128 (bus
stop); Photodisc / OUPpicturebank, pg. 128 (playing baseball); Ingram /
OUPpicturebank, pg. 128 (studying); Blend Images / OUPpicturebank, pg.
128 (cooking); Stockbyte / OUPpicturebank, pg. 128 (playing guitar); OUP /
OUPpicturebank, pg. 134; Alex James Bramwell / Shutterstock,
pg. 135; Dex Image / OUPpicturebank, pg. 145 (mechanic); Digital Vision
/ OUPpicturebank, pg. 145 (chef); Trevor Smithers / OUPpicturebank,
pg. 145 (tour guide); CandyBoxPhoto / Shutterstock, pg. 145 (optician);
Digital Vision / OUPpicturebank, pg. 145 (professor); Corbis / Digital
Stock / OUPpicturebank, pg. 145 (surgeon); Photodisc / OUPpicturebank,
pg. 155 (woman); Antonio Jorge Nunes / Shutterstock, pg. 155 (man (l));
OUP / OUPpicturebank, pg. 155 (man (r)); ARENA Creative / Shutterstock,
pg. 158; Digital Vision / OUPpicturebank, pg. 163; ylq / Shutterstock,
pg. 170; Panos Karapanagiotis / Shutterstock, pg. 174; GTS Production
/ Shutterstock, pg. 175 (Cleopatra); OUP / OUPpicturebank, pg. 175
(Columbus); Pictorial Press Ltd / Alamy, pg. 175 (Albert Einstein); Bettmann
/ Corbis, pg. 185 (1770s French hairstyle); Hulton Collection / Getty Images,
pg. 185 (lady in dress); Bettmann / Corbis, pg. 204 (Chicago after Great
Fire); Bettmann / Corbis, pg. 205 (Boston Molasses Disaster); Corbis /
OUPpicturebank, pg. 209; Hulton-Deutsch / Corbis, pg. 212; Deklofenak
/ Shutterstock, pg. 214 (men at lunch); Stockbyte / OUPpicturebank,
pg. 214 (men playing basketball); BananaStock / OUPpicturebank, pg.
214 (man on phone); Jess Yu / Shutterstock, pg. 214 (student in library);
Cultura Creative / Alamy, pg. 214 (men jogging); lightpoet / Shutterstock,
pg. 214 (students taking test); Photodisc / OUPpicturebank, pg. 220 (taxi);
Nigel Reed QEDimages / OUPpicturebank, pg. 220 (museum); Digital
Vision / OUPpicturebank, pg. 221; Justin Kase / OUPpicturebank, pg. 223;
Ronnie Kaufman / Corbis, pg. 232; Stephen Coburn / Shutterstock, pg.
239; Deco / OUPpicturebank, pg. 243 (city); Colin Palmer Photography /
OUPpicturebank, pg. 243 (town); Photodisc / OUPpicturebank, pg. 266
(baseball); Alessio Ponti / Shutterstock, pg. 266 (soccer); Aspen Photo /
Shutterstock, pg. 267; Fuse / OUPpicturebank, pg. 276 (airplane); Mika
Heittola / Shutterstock, pg. 276 (skater); vahamrick / Shutterstock, pg. 276
(dinner); Anderson Ross / Blend Images / Corbis, pg. 276 (children); sonya
etchison / Shutterstock, pg. 276 (school bus); Photodisc / OUPpicturebank,
pg. 276 (baseball batter); Blend Images / Alamy, pg. 280; INSADCO
Photography / Alamy, pg. 281; Liz Boyd / OUPpicturebank, pg. 288; Yuri
Arcurs / Shutterstock, pg. 295 (man (l)); olly / Shutterstock, pg. 295 (man
(r)); Boudikka / Shutterstock, pg. 306; Fancy / OUPpicturebank, pg. 311;
Maridav / Shutterstock, pg. 314; Kevin Peterson / OUPpicturebank, pg.
318; SVLuma / Shutterstock, pg. 332; Lifesize / OUPpicturebank, pg. 340
(student running); Blend Images / Alamy, pg. 340 (student eating); Jose Gil
/ Shutterstock, pg. 346; Author's Image / OUPpicturebank, pg. 347; Image
Source / OUPpicturebank, pg. 361; gh19 / Shutterstock, pg. 363; auremar
/ Shutterstock, pg. 368; OUP / OUPpicturebank, pg. 374 (cell phone);
Jason Brindel Commercial / OUPpicturebank, pg. 374 (smartphone);
StockLite / Shutterstock, pg. 375; Ingram / OUPpicturebank, pg. 381 (bike);
Margo Harrison / Shutterstock, pg. 381 (motorcycle); Nicholas Piccillo /
Shutterstock, pg. 381 (football player); Yuri Arcurs / Shutterstock, pg. 381
(basketball player); Juniors Bildarchiv / OUPpicturebank, pg. 381 (bird);
Photodisc / OUPpicturebank, pg. 381 (cat); Seregam / Shutterstock, pg. 387.

Reviewers

We would like to acknowledge the following individuals for their input during the development of the series:

Marcia Adato, Delaware Technical and Community College, DE
Donette Artenie, Georgetown University, DC
Alexander Astor, Hostos Community College/CUNY, Bronx, NY
Nathalie Bailey, Lehman College, CUNY, NY
Jamie Beaton, Boston University, MA
Michael Berman, Montgomery College, MD
Linda Best, Kean University, NJ
Marcel Bolintiam, Kings Colleges, Los Angeles, CA
Houda Bouslama, Virtual University Tunis, Tunis, Tunisia
Nancy Boyer, Golden West College, Huntington Beach, CA
Glenda Bro, Mount San Antonio Community College, CA
Shannonine Caruana, Kean University, NJ
Sharon Cavusgil, Georgia State University, GA
Robin Rosen Chang, Kean University, NJ
Jorge Cordon, Colegio Internacional Montessori, Guatemala
Magali Duignan, Augusta State University, GA
Anne Ediger, Hunter College, CUNY, NY
Begoña Escourdio, Colegio Miraflores, Naucalpan, Mexico
Marcella Farina, University of Central Florida, FL
Carol Fox, Oakton Community College, Niles, IL
Glenn S. Gardner, Glendale Community College, Glendale, CA
Ruth Griffith, Kean University, NJ
Evalyn Hansen, Rogue Community College, Medford, OR
Liz Hardy, Rogue Community College, Medford, OR
Habiba Hassina, Virtual University Tunis, Tunis, Tunisia
Virginia Heringer, Pasadena City College, CA
Rocia Hernandez, Mexico City, Mexico
Kieran Hilu, Virginia Tech, VA
Rosemary Hiruma, California State University, Long Beach, CA
Linda Holden, College of Lake County, Grayslake, IL
Elke Holtz, Escuela Sierra Nevada Interlomas, Mexico City, Mexico
Kate de Jong, University of California, San Diego, CA
Gail Kellersberger, University of Houston-Downtown, ELI, Houston, TX

Pamela Kennedy, Holyoke Community College, MA
Elis Lee, Glendale Community College, Glendale, CA
Patricia Lowy, State University of New York-New Paltz, NY
Jean McConochie, Pace University, NY
Karen McRobie, Golden Gate University, CA
Hafid Mekaoui, Al Akhawayn University, Ifrane, Morocco
Elizabeth Neblett, Union County College, NJ
Patricia Palermo, Kean University, NJ
Maria E. Palma, Colegio Lationamericano Bilingue, Chihuahua, Mexico
Mary Peacock, Richland College, Dallas, TX
Dian Perkins, Wheeling High School, IL
Nancy Herzfeld-Pipkin, Grossmont College, El Cajon, CA
Kent Richmond, California State University, Long Beach, CA
Ellen Rosen, Fullerton College, CA
Jessica Saigh, University of Missouri-St. Louis, St. Louis, MO
Boutheina Lassadi-Sayadi, The Faculty of Humanities and Social Sciences of Tunis, Tunis, Tunisia
Anne-Marie Schlender, Austin Community College-Rio Grande, Austin, TX
Shira Seaman, Global English Academy, NY
Katharine Sherak, San Francisco State University, CA
Maxine Steinhaus, New York University, NY
Andrea Stewart, Houston Community College-Gulfton, Houston, TX
Nancy Storer, University of Denver, CO
Veronica Struck, Sussex Community College, Newton, NJ
Frank Tang, New York University, NY
Claude Taylor, Baruch College, NY
Marshall Thomas, California State University, Long Beach, CA
Christine Tierney, Houston Community College, Houston, TX
Anthea Tillyer, Hunter College, CUNY, NY
Julie Un, Massasoit Community College, MA
Marvaette Washington, Houston Community College, Houston, TX
Cheryl Wecksler, California State University, San Marcos, CA
Teresa Wise, Associated Colleges of the South, GA

Contents

Welcome to Grammar Sense

A Sensible Solution to Learning Grammar

Grammar Sense Second Edition gives learners a true understanding of how grammar is used in authentic contexts.

 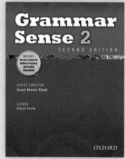 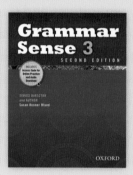 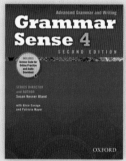

With Grammar Sense Online Practice

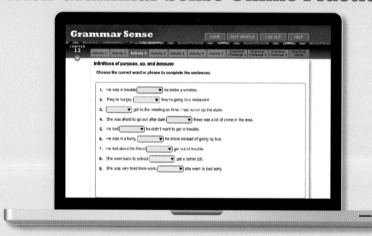

- **Student Solutions:** a **focus on Critical Thinking** for improved application of grammatical knowledge.

- **Writing Solutions:** a **Writing section in every chapter** encourages students to see the relevance of grammar in their writing.

- **Technology Solutions:** *Grammar Sense Online Practice* provides additional practice in an easy-to-use **online workbook**.

- **Assessment Solutions:** the Part Tests at the end of every section and the Grammar Sense Test Generators allow **ongoing assessment**.

Each chapter in *Grammar Sense Second Edition* **follows** this format.

The Grammar in Discourse section introduces the target grammar in its natural context via high-interest readings.

> **Pre- and post-reading tasks** help students understand the text.

A GRAMMAR IN DISCOURSE

What Kind of Learner Are You?

A1 Before You Read

Discuss these questions.

Do you like to listen to lectures? Do you prefer to look at pictures and diagrams? Do you like to do experiments? Do you think everyone learns in the same way?

A2 Read

 CD1 T43 Read the article from a science magazine on the following page. What kind of learner are you?

A3 After You Read

Write *T* for true or *F* for false for each statement.

___T___ 1. Teachers like good listeners.

_____ 2. Good listeners don't always follow instructions.

_____ 3. Julie Hong does well in school.

_____ 4. Larry D

_____ 5. Hands-

_____ 6. Pete D

> Exposure to **authentic readings** encourages awareness of the grammar in daily life: in textbooks, magazines, newspapers, websites, and so on.

▶ SCIENCE MAGAZINE

What Kind of Learner Are You?

Researchers say that there are at least three different types of learners.

Some learners are good listeners. Teachers like them because they always
5 follow instructions. Julie Hong is a student like this. She gets A's in all her classes at Deerfield High School in
10 Connecticut. She loves school, and her teachers love her because she always pays attention in class. "I pay attention because I don't want to miss important information," she says.

15 Some people learn from pictures and diagrams. They are very creative but don't like details.
20 Larry Dawson is a good example of this kind of learner. He is studying graphic design at Warfield Community College in Ohio. He is usually

25 very good with ideas and concepts but sometimes has problems with details. "New ideas are exciting, but I often get bored at the end of a big project," Larry admits.

Some learners
30 rarely learn from books or pictures. They are "hands-on" learners. They learn from
35 experience. Pete Donaldson is a good example of a hands-on learner. Pete is studying computer science at the University of Florida. Pete never reads
40 computer manuals and seldom looks at diagrams. He just spends hours on the computer. "That's the best way for me to learn," he says.

So, what kind of learner are you?
45 Do you always learn the same way? Or do you learn one way in some classes and another way in others?

The Form section(s) provides clear presentation of the target grammar, detailed notes, and thorough practice exercises.

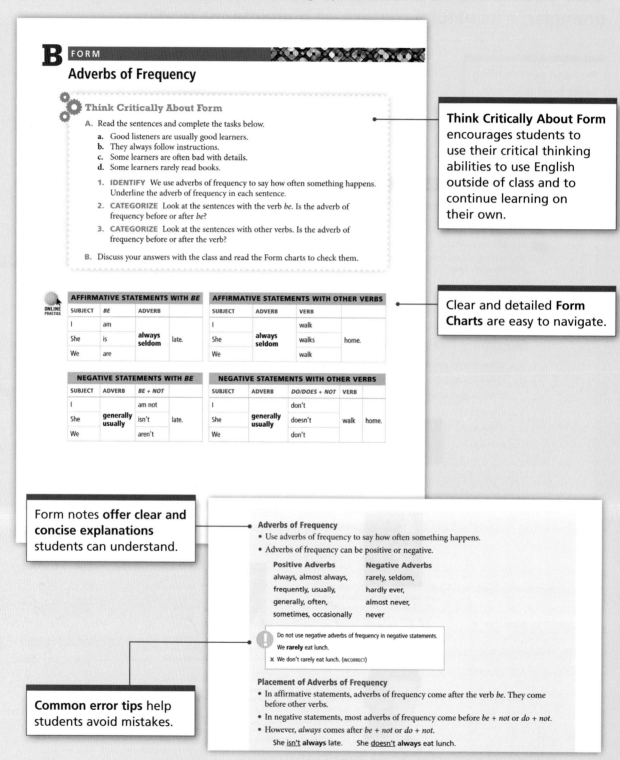

B FORM

Adverbs of Frequency

Think Critically About Form

A. Read the sentences and complete the tasks below.

a. Good listeners are usually good learners.
b. They always follow instructions.
c. Some learners are often bad with details.
d. Some learners rarely read books.

1. **IDENTIFY** We use adverbs of frequency to say how often something happens. Underline the adverb of frequency in each sentence.
2. **CATEGORIZE** Look at the sentences with the verb *be*. Is the adverb of frequency before or after *be*?
3. **CATEGORIZE** Look at the sentences with other verbs. Is the adverb of frequency before or after the verb?

B. Discuss your answers with the class and read the Form charts to check them.

> **Think Critically About Form** encourages students to use their critical thinking abilities to use English outside of class and to continue learning on their own.

ONLINE PRACTICE

AFFIRMATIVE STATEMENTS WITH BE

SUBJECT	BE	ADVERB	
I	am		
She	is	**always seldom**	late.
We	are		

AFFIRMATIVE STATEMENTS WITH OTHER VERBS

SUBJECT	ADVERB	VERB	
I		walk	
She	**always seldom**	walks	home.
We		walk	

> Clear and detailed **Form Charts** are easy to navigate.

NEGATIVE STATEMENTS WITH BE

SUBJECT	ADVERB	BE + NOT	
I		am not	
She	**generally usually**	isn't	late.
We		aren't	

NEGATIVE STATEMENTS WITH OTHER VERBS

SUBJECT	ADVERB	DO/DOES + NOT	VERB	
I		don't		
She	**generally usually**	doesn't	walk	home.
We		don't		

> Form notes **offer clear and concise explanations** students can understand.

Adverbs of Frequency
- Use adverbs of frequency to say how often something happens.
- Adverbs of frequency can be positive or negative.

Positive Adverbs	Negative Adverbs
always, almost always,	rarely, seldom,
frequently, usually,	hardly ever,
generally, often,	almost never,
sometimes, occasionally	never

> **!** Do not use negative adverbs of frequency in negative statements.
> We **rarely** eat lunch.
> ✗ We don't rarely eat lunch. (INCORRECT)

Placement of Adverbs of Frequency
- In affirmative statements, adverbs of frequency come after the verb *be*. They come before other verbs.
- In negative statements, most adverbs of frequency come before *be + not* or *do + not*.
- However, *always* comes after *be + not* or *do + not*.
  > She <u>isn't</u> **always** late.   She <u>doesn't</u> **always** eat lunch.

> **Common error tips** help students avoid mistakes.

The Meaning and Use section(s) offers clear and comprehensive explanations of how the target structure is used, and exercises to practice using it appropriately.

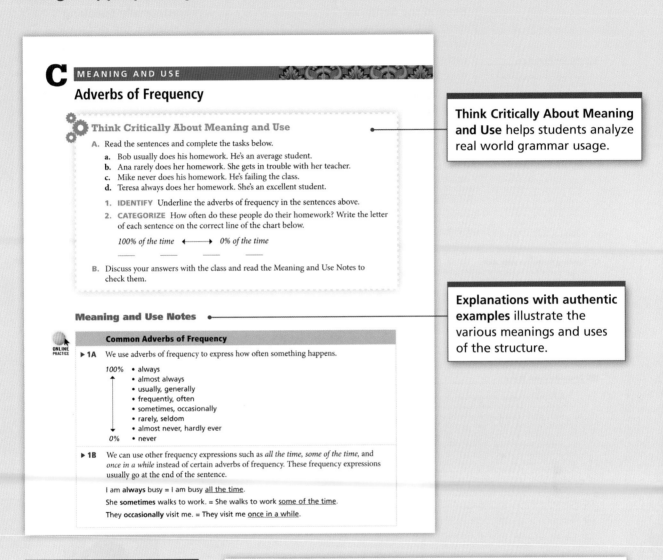

C MEANING AND USE

Adverbs of Frequency

Think Critically About Meaning and Use

A. Read the sentences and complete the tasks below.
  a. Bob usually does his homework. He's an average student.
  b. Ana rarely does her homework. She gets in trouble with her teacher.
  c. Mike never does his homework. He's failing the class.
  d. Teresa always does her homework. She's an excellent student.

  1. **IDENTIFY** Underline the adverbs of frequency in the sentences above.
  2. **CATEGORIZE** How often do these people do their homework? Write the letter of each sentence on the correct line of the chart below.

     100% of the time ◄─────► 0% of the time
     ____   ____

B. Discuss your answers with the class and read the Meaning and Use Notes to check them.

Think Critically About Meaning and Use helps students analyze real world grammar usage.

Meaning and Use Notes

ONLINE PRACTICE

Common Adverbs of Frequency

▶ **1A** We use adverbs of frequency to express how often something happens.

  100% • always
        • almost always
        • usually, generally
        • frequently, often
        • sometimes, occasionally
        • rarely, seldom
        • almost never, hardly ever
  0%   • never

▶ **1B** We can use other frequency expressions such as *all the time*, *some of the time*, and *once in a while* instead of certain adverbs of frequency. These frequency expressions usually go at the end of the sentence.

  I am **always** busy = I am busy <u>all the time</u>.
  She **sometimes** walks to work. = She walks to work <u>some of the time</u>.
  They **occasionally** visit me. = They visit me <u>once in a while</u>.

Explanations with authentic examples illustrate the various meanings and uses of the structure.

Practice exercises enable students to use the grammar structure appropriately and fluently.

C1 Listening for Meaning and Use   ▶ Notes 1A–3A

CD1 T45 Listen to Mark and Erica's conversation. Check (✓) the correct column.

	Mark	Erica
1. looks at diagrams	____	✓
2. follows instructions well	____	____
3. doesn't usually make things	____	____
4. frequently cooks	____	____
5. rarely collects recipes	____	____
6. usually fixes things.	____	____

Special sections appear throughout the chapters with clear explanations, authentic examples, and follow-up exercises.

Beyond the Sentence demonstrates how structures function differently in extended discourses.

Informally Speaking clarifies the differences between written and spoken language.

Beyond the Sentence

Combining Sentences with *And*

We can use *and* to combine sentences. Use a comma to combine two complete sentences.

I am taking a shower. Alex is making dinner.

I am taking a shower, **and** Alex is making dinner.

When two affirmative present continuous sentences have the same subject, we usually don't repeat the subject or *am/is/are*. In this case, we do not use a comma.

He is doing his homework. He <u>is watching</u> television.

He is doing his homework **and** <u>watching</u> television.

When we write, we combine sentences because it makes our writing sound more natural. Compare these two paragraphs.

A.

Everyone in my family is very busy. My father is working out of town during the week. My father is coaching a soccer team on the weekends. My mother is teaching at the university. My mother is trying to start her own business. My brother Josh is going to law school. My brother Josh is working at a law firm.

B.

Everyone in my family is very busy. My father is working out of town during the week **and** coaching a soccer team on the weekends. My mother is teaching at the university **and** trying to start her own business. My brother Josh is going to law school **and** working at a law firm.

C5 Combing Sentences with *And*

Rewrite the paragraph in your notebook. Use *and* to combine the underlined sentences. Punctuate your sentences correctly.

Dear Luisa,

Thanks for your letter. We're very busy, too. <u>We're working hard. We're saving money.</u> <u>Celia is teaching piano at the local high school. She's giving private lessons on the weekends.</u> <u>I'm finishing my Ph.D. I'm writing my dissertation.</u> Right now, <u>Celia is making dinner. Our daughter Lucy is helping her…</u>

Informally Speaking

Contractions with *Wh-* Word + *Be*

CD1 T11 Look at the cartoon and listen to the conversation. How is the underlined form in the cartoon different from what you hear?

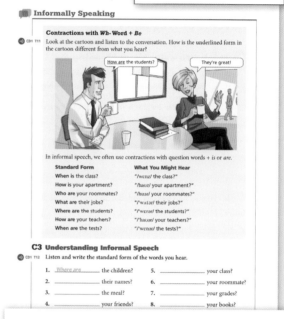

How <u>are</u> the students?

They're great!

In informal speech, we often use contractions with question words + *is* or *are*.

Standard Form	What You Might Hear
When is the class?	"/wɛnz/ the class?"
How is your apartment?	"/haʊz/ your apartment?"
Who are your roommates?	"/huər/ your roommates?"
What are their jobs?	"/wʌtər/ their jobs?"
Where are the students?	"/wɛrər/ the students?"
How are your teachers?	"/haʊər/ your teachers?"
When are the tests?	"/wɛnər/ the tests?"

C3 Understanding Informal Speech

CD1 T12 Listen and write the standard form of the words you hear.

1. _Where are_ the children?
2. _____ their names?
3. _____ the meal?
4. _____ your friends?
5. _____ your class?
6. _____ your roommate?
7. _____ your grades?
8. _____ your books?

Pronunciation Notes

Pronunciation of Regular Plural Nouns

We pronounce the final sound of regular plural nouns in three different ways.

1. As /s/ after the voiceless sounds /p/, /t/, /k/, /f/, and /θ/.

   caps   apartments   packs   cliffs   months

2. As /ɪz/ after the sounds /dʒ/, /tʃ/, /s/, /z/, /ʃ/, /ʒ/, and /ks/.

   bridges   watches   classes   quizzes   dishes   garages   boxes

3. As /z/ after all other sounds.

   doctors   employees   kitchens   words   lives

C4 Pronouncing Regular Plural Nouns

CD1 T20 A. Listen to each plural noun. What ending do you hear? Check (✓) the correct column.

		/s/	/ɪz/	/z/
1.	cars	✓		
2.	pencils			
3.	wishes			
4.	roommates			
5.	nouns			
6.	maps			

B. Work with a partner. Take turns pronouncing the pairs of words below. Choose the correct sound for the plural ending.

1. road — roads   /s/ /ɪz/ /z/
2. clock — clocks   /s/ /ɪz/ /z/
3. belief — beliefs   /s/ /ɪz/ /z/
4. room — rooms   /s/ /ɪz/ /z/
5. sentence — sentences   /s/ /ɪz/ /z/
6. excuse — excuses   /s/ /ɪz/ /z/
7. garage — garages   /s/ /ɪz/ /z/
8. apartment — apartments   /s/ /ɪz/ /z/

Pronunciation Notes show students how to pronounce forms of the target language.

Vocabulary Notes

How Often … ? and Frequency Expressions

Use *How often … ?* to ask about frequency. We often use frequency expressions to answer questions with *How often … ?*

every day/night/afternoon/Saturday	twice a year/week
once a day/week/month/year	three times a day/month

A: **How often** do you exercise?   A: **How often** do you clean your apartment?

B: (I exercise) **every day**.   B: (I clean my apartment) **once a week**.

C4 Asking Questions About Frequency

A. Work with a partner. Take turns asking and answering questions about the things on the list. Ask questions with *How often … ?* Answer with frequency expressions. Take notes on your partner's responses.

1. talk on your cell phone

   A: *How often do you talk on your cell phone?*
   B: *Five times a day.*

2. shop for clothes
3. have lunch with your friends
4. go to a bookstore
5. study in the library
6. visit your family
7. take a bus
8. do your laundry

B. Now tell the class about your partner.

Luisa talks on her cell phone five times a day.

Vocabulary Notes highlight the connection between the key vocabulary and grammatical structures.

The Writing section guides students through the process of applying grammatical knowledge to compositions.

WRITING   Write About Your Learning Style

 Think Critically About Meaning and Use

A. Complete each conversation.

1. A: Jack always does his homework on time.

   B: Yes. _____
   a. He's a good student.
   b. He rarely studies.
   c. He seldom works hard.

2. A: I'm frequently late for work.

   B: _____
   a. Do you need a new alarm clock?
   b. Does this happen often?
   c. Are you ever late?

3. A: Do you often take vacations?

   B: No. _____
   a. We sometimes do.
   b. We rarely do.
   c. We always do.

4. A: This bus never comes on time.

   B: I know. _____
   a. It's never late.
   b. It's usually on time.
   c. It's always late.

B. Discuss these questions in small groups.

1. **GENERATE** Look at 1. Speaker B wants to use *never* in the response. What would he or she say?

2. **GENERATE** Look at 2. Imagine you are speaker B. Can you think of 2–3 other responses to A's statement?

Edit

Some of these sentences have errors. Find the errors and correct them.

1. always
   Ålways Lisa is late.

2. He gets up rarely on time.

3. She seldom hears her alarm clock.

4. How often you call home?

> Integrating grammar into the writing process helps students **see the relevance of grammar to their own writing**.

> Editing exercises focus students on **identifying and correcting problems** in sentence structure and usage.

Write

Write a paragraph about your own learning style. Use adverbs of frequency.

1. **BRAINSTORM** List different things that make learning easier for you. Use these questions to help you.
   - What type of learner are you?
   - What types of learning do you enjoy?
   - What things do you find easy or difficult to do?
   - What do you do to remember things?

2. **WRITE A FIRST DRAFT** Write a draft using adverbs of frequency and the simple present tense. Before you write your first draft, read the checklist below and look at the example on page 155. Write your draft using adverbs of frequency.

3. **EDIT** Read your work and check it against the checklist below. Circle grammar, spelling, and punctuation errors.

DO I ...	YES
use adverbs of frequency?	☐
use positive and negative adverbs?	☐
use simple present tense?	☐
use adverbs in the correct position?	☐
use the adverb *ever* at least one time?	☐
use adverbs that show opposites at least one time?	☐

4. **PEER REVIEW** Work with a partner to help you decide how to fix your errors and improve the content.

5. **REWRITE YOUR DRAFT** Using the comments from your partner, write a final draft.

> Collaborating with classmates in **peer review** helps students improve their own grammar skills.

Assessment

> **Part Tests** allow ongoing assessment and evaluate the students' mastery of the grammar.

Teacher's Resources

Teacher's Book

- Creative techniques for presenting the grammar, along with troubleshooting tips, and suggestions for additional activities

- Answer key and audio scripts

- Includes a *Grammar Sense Online Practice* Teacher Access Code

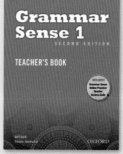

Class Audio

- Audio CDs feature exercises for discriminating form, understanding meaning and use, and interpreting non-standard forms

Test Generator CD-ROM

- Over 3,000 items available!

- Test-generating software allows you to customize tests for all levels of Grammar Sense

- Includes a bank of ready-made tests

Grammar Sense Teachers' Club site contains additional teaching resources at www.oup.com/elt/teacher/grammarsense

ONLINE PRACTICE

Grammar Sense Online Practice is an online program with all new content. It correlates with the *Grammar Sense* student books and provides additional practice.

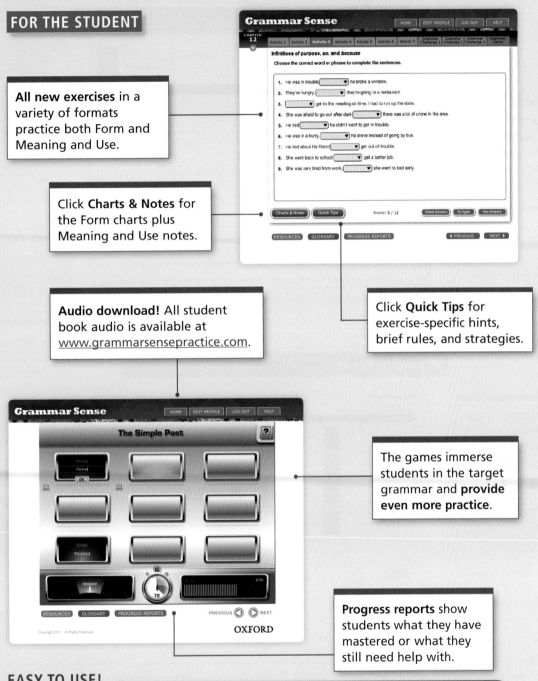

All new exercises in a variety of formats practice both Form and Meaning and Use.

Click **Charts & Notes** for the Form charts plus Meaning and Use notes.

Audio download! All student book audio is available at www.grammarsensepractice.com.

Click **Quick Tips** for exercise-specific hints, brief rules, and strategies.

The games immerse students in the target grammar and **provide even more practice**.

Progress reports show students what they have mastered or what they still need help with.

EASY TO USE!

Use the access code printed on the inside back cover of this book to register at www.grammarsensepractice.com. See the last page of the book for registration instructions.

Flexible enough for use in the classroom or easily assigned as homework.

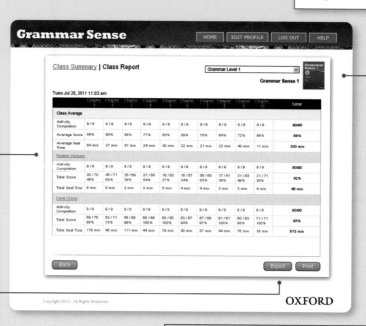

Grammar Sense Online Practice **automatically grades** student exercises and tracks progress.

The easy-to-use online management system allows you to **review, print, or export** the reports you need.

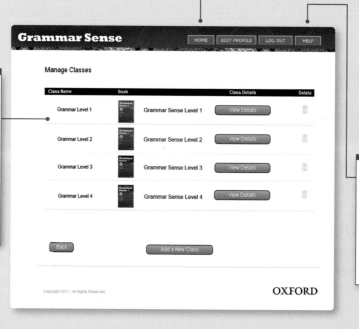

The **straightforward online management system** allows you to add or delete classes, manage your classes, plus view, print, or export all class and individual student reports.

You can **access all** *Grammar Sense Online Practice* **activities,** download the student book audio, and utilize the additional student resources.

Click Help for simple, step-by-step support that is **available in six languages**: English, Spanish, Korean, Arabic, Chinese, and Japanese.

FOR ADDITIONAL SUPPORT
Email our customer support team at grammarsensesupport@oup.com and you will receive a response within 24 hours.

FOR ADMNISTRATOR CODES
Please contact your sales representative for an Administrator Access Code. A Teacher Access Code comes with every Teacher's Book.

PART

6

Articles;
Quantity
Expressions;
There Is and
There Are

CHAPTER

14

Articles

How to Enjoy a New City

A1 Before You Read

Discuss these questions.

Do you like visiting new cities? Why or why not? What is your favorite city? What is interesting about it?

A2 Read

 CD2 T2 Read the magazine article on the following page about moving to a new city. What suggestions does it make?

A3 After You Read

Write *T* for true or *F* for false for each statement.

__T__ **1.** It's sometimes hard to meet people in a big city.

_____ **2.** It's a good idea to carry a map of the city.

_____ **3.** It's a good idea to talk to local people.

_____ **4.** It's not a good idea to use public transportation.

_____ **5.** It's not a good idea to talk to taxi drivers.

_____ **6.** It's a good idea to eat in ethnic neighborhoods.

Taxi drivers know a lot about their city.

Museums are good places to visit.

HOW TO ENJOY A NEW CITY

For some people, a new city is exciting. For other people, however, a move to a new city can be difficult. Cities are big places and sometimes it's hard to meet people. Here are a few ways to get to know a new city and its people.

Buy a guidebook before you get to the city. Read the guidebook in your free time. Look for interesting places to go.

When you get there, buy a city map. Keep the map in your pocket or purse. Look at the map and find a park. Buy a newspaper and read it in the park, or just watch the people. Look back at the guidebook. Find the interesting places on your map. Make plans to visit them.

Buy a bus map. On sunny days, ride buses and look out a window. With the bus map and your guidebook, it is easy to travel around the city. Talk to people. A bus stop is a very good place for a conversation with a stranger.

Taxi drivers know a lot about their city. Take taxis and talk to the drivers. Ask them about ethnic neighborhoods in the city. Visit the neighborhoods. Walk around for an hour or two. Shop in the stores. Find a good ethnic restaurant and eat delicious new food.

Think about your special interests. Are you a sports fan? Find a sports stadium or arena. Buy a ticket to a game. Go to the game and start a conversation with other fans. Are you interested in museums? Choose a museum. Spend a few hours in the museum on a rainy day.

---

arena: an enclosed area for sporting events
ethnic: connected with a particular culture

guidebook: a book for tourists with information about interesting places
stadium: a large building used for sports events

B FORM

Indefinite and Definite Articles

Think Critically About Form

A. Read the sentences and complete the tasks below.

a. Buy a map. Take the map with you.
b. Do you like art? Visit a museum.
c. Take taxis and talk to the drivers.
d. Ethnic food is delicious. Try the food in ethnic restaurants.

1. **IDENTIFY** Underline the count nouns in the sentences. Circle the noncount nouns.

2. **APPLY** When do we use the article *a* or *an*? When do we use the article *the*? When do we use no article (Ø)? Check (✓) the correct columns in the chart below.

	A/AN	*THE*	*Ø*
before singular count nouns			
before plural count nouns			
before noncount nouns			

B. Discuss your answers with the class and read the Form charts to check them.

INDEFINITE ARTICLE	
A/AN	**SINGULAR COUNT NOUN**
a	city
an	hour evening

DEFINITE ARTICLE	
THE	**SINGULAR COUNT NOUN**
the	city hour evening

Ø	**PLURAL COUNT NOUN**
	cities hours evenings

THE	**PLURAL COUNT NOUN**
the	cities hours evenings

Ø	**NONCOUNT NOUN**
	information milk work

THE	**NONCOUNT NOUN**
the	information milk work

Indefinite Articles

- The indefinite article is *a* or *an*.
- Use the indefinite article before a singular count noun *(a man)* or before an adjective + singular count noun *(a tall man)*.
- Use *a* before words that begin with a consonant sound. Use *an* before words that begin with a vowel sound.
- Use no article (Ø) before plural count nouns and noncount nouns.

Definite Articles

- The definite article is *the*.
- Use the definite article before singular and plural count nouns, and noncount nouns.
- Use the definite article before a noun *(the man)* or an adjective + noun *(the tall man)*.

B1 Listening for Form

CD2 T3   Paul was in Paris last year. Listen to Paul talk about his experiences. Write the article you hear. Use Ø for no article. Use a capital letter when needed.

Paris is __an__ exciting city. It is ___ great city to visit. I spent ___ time there last
          1   2   3
year. I liked ___ museums best. My favorite museum was the Musée d'Orsay. This
              4
museum is in ___ old train station. ___ station closed in 1939. ___ museum opened
             5   6   7
in 1986. It has ___ famous paintings and sculptures. It was ___ wonderful place to
                8   9
spend ___ afternoon.
      10

The interior of the Musée d'Orsay

B2 Forming Sentences with *A/An* or No Article

Form sentences with the words and phrases. Use *a, an,* or no article with the underlined words. Punctuate your sentences correctly.

1. I/left/<u>sweater</u>/at your house

   I left a sweater at your house.

2. I/love/<u>Thai food</u>

3. he/is working/on/<u>university degree</u>

4. Celia/bought/<u>new furniture</u>

5. my friends/rented/<u>house</u>/in San Antonio

6. My husband/is/<u>wonderful man</u>

7. <u>guidebook</u>/is/<u>book</u>/for tourists

8. Keiko/doesn't like/<u>museums</u>

9. Paris/is/<u>beautiful city</u>

10. <u>new cars</u>/are/expensive

B3 Working with Indefinite and Definite Articles

Rewrite each phrase with *a* or *an* if possible. Write ✗ where no change is possible.

1. the old man *an old man*
2. the boy _____
3. the information _____
6. the answer _____
7. the new store _____
8. the woman _____

B4 Choosing the Correct Article

Choose the correct article or articles. More than one answer may be possible.

1. Please buy ____ apples.

   a. a   **b.** an   **c.** ∅

2. Juan loves ____ classical music.

   a. a   **b.** an   **c.** ∅

3. It was late, but ____ stores were still open.

   a. a   **b.** the   **c.** ∅

4. Susan loves ____ modern art.

   a. a   **b.** an   **c.** ∅

5. ____ Italian restaurants in New York are fantastic.

   a. An   **b.** The   **c.** ∅

6. Take ____ taxi to the airport.

   a. a   **b.** the   **c.** ∅

7. They serve ____ delicious food there.

   a. a   **b.** an   **c.** ∅

8. ____ teacher asked my name.

   a. A   **b.** The   **c.** ∅

C MEANING AND USE

Indefinite and Definite Articles

Think Critically About Meaning and Use

A. Read the sentences and answer the questions below.

a. I saw a great movie last night.
b. The movie was interesting.
c. It was about an English soldier.
d. The soldier lost his memory.

1. **IDENTIFY** Underline the article and noun in each sentence.

2. **CATEGORIZE** Which sentences introduce a noun for the first time?

3. **CATEGORIZE** Which sentences mention the noun for the second time?

B. Discuss your answers with the class and read the Meaning and Use Notes to check them.

Meaning and Use Notes

ONLINE PRACTICE

Introducing a Noun

▶ 1A Use *a, an,* or no article to introduce a noun for the first time. The speaker has a specific noun in mind. The listener does not.

A: I have **a new apartment**.

B: Where is it?

A: I have **new jeans**.

B: And I have **new shoes**!

A: Do you want to hear **a joke**?

B: Sure. Go right ahead.

▶ 1B Sometimes the speaker does not have a specific noun in mind either.

A: I'm looking for **a new car**, but I don't know what kind.

B: Are you looking for **a big car** or **a small car**?

Mentioning a Noun for the Second Time

▶ **2** Use *the* to talk about a noun for the second time (after you introduce the noun).

In a Newspaper

Local investors built <u>a new factory</u> in Jamestown. **The factory** opened last week.

Customer to a Computer Repair Person

A: I bought <u>new software</u>, but it doesn't work.

B: Who installed **the software**?

At the Office

A: I had <u>a sandwich</u> and <u>soup</u> for lunch.

B: How was **the soup**?

Shared Information

▶ **3** Use *the* when the speaker and the listener have a specific noun in mind because they share common information.

Father to Son

Please wash **the car**.

Boss to Employee

Have you finished **the report**?

C1 Listening for Meaning and Use
▶ Notes 1A–2

CD2 T4   **Look at the chart. Listen to the conversation. Is each noun mentioned for the first time or the second time? Check (✓) the correct column.**

		FIRST MENTION	SECOND MENTION
1.	vacation	✓	
2.	trip		
3.	tour		
4.	tour		
5.	guide		
6.	trip		
7.	accident		
8.	park		

C2 Using Indefinite and Definite Articles

▶ Notes 1A–3

Complete the conversations. Use *a, an, the,* or no article (Ø). Use a capital letter when needed.

1. **A:** Do you like __Ø__ pets?

    ₁

    B: Yes, I do. I have _____ rabbit and _____ cat. _____ rabbit isn't very intelligent, but

    ₂   ₃   ₄

    _____ cat is very smart.

    ₅

2. **A:** Where are _____ car keys, Michael? I'm late for work.

    ₁

    B: Oh, I saw them on _____ kitchen table about _____ hour ago.

    ₂   ₃

3. **A:** Do you need _____ help?

    ₁

    B: Yes. I'm looking for _____ suit.

    ₂

    A: Do you want _____ business suit or _____ casual suit?

    ₃   ₄

C3 Contrasting Indefinite and Definite Articles

▶ Note 3

A. Complete the conversations. Use *a, an,* or *the.*

NS 1. **A:** Would you like __a__ salad with your sandwich?

    B: No, thanks. I'm not very hungry.

_____ 2. **A:** Don't forget to lock _____ door.

    B: Don't worry, Mom.

_____ 3. **A:** The car is making a funny noise!

    B: We need _____ new car!

_____ 4. **A:** Susan, did you take _____ contract to Mr. Ruiz's office?

    B: No, I'm working on it right now.

_____ 5. **A:** _____ TV is too loud. Please close your door.

    B: Sure. No problem.

B. Look at the underlined noun in each conversation in part A. Does the speaker have a specific noun or a nonspecific noun in mind? Write *S* for specific or *NS* for nonspecific.

WRITING   Write About a City You Enjoy

Think Critically About Meaning and Use

A. Complete each conversation.

1. A: What is _____ good present for
   Ana?

   B: Buy her a CD.

   (a.) a

   b. an

   c. the

2. A: Do you like _____ classical
   music?

   B: Well, I prefer pop music.

   a. Ø

   b. the

   c. a

3. A: These eggs are delicious.

   B: _____ recipe is really easy.

   a. Ø

   b. A

   c. The

4. A: I'm really hungry. Let's buy
   lunch.

   B: Do you want _____ sandwich?

   a. Ø

   b. the

   c. a

B. Discuss these questions in small groups.

1. **EVALUATE**   In 1, imagine A asks: "Which one of these two presents is good for
   Ana?" In response, B says: "Buy her ____ CD." What word completes B's sentence?

2. **EXPLAIN**   In 3, why does B's answer begin with *the* and not *a*?

Edit

Some of these sentences have errors. Find the errors and correct them.

1. Buy ~~an~~ *a* map.

2. Prague is the wonderful city.

3. Is a telephone call for me?

4. Please put a stamp on this letter.

5. Museums are fun on the rainy days.

6. My uncle is a policeman.

Write

Update your blog with some advice about a city you visited and really liked. Use definite and indefinite articles.

1. **BRAINSTORM** Think of a city you want to write about and list all the features that a visitor should know about. Use the following questions to help you organize your thoughts.

   - What do readers need to know before they visit this city? What should they bring?
   - What kind of tourist sights are there in this city: museums, parks, sports stadiums? Which is your favorite?
   - What kind of public transportation do people use?
   - Which restaurants do you recommend?
   - What else would a visitor like to do in this place?

2. **WRITE A FIRST DRAFT** Before you write your first draft, read the checklist below and look at the example on page 223. Write your draft using a mixture of definite and indefinite articles.

3. **EDIT** Read your work and check it against the checklist below. Circle grammar, spelling, and punctuation errors.

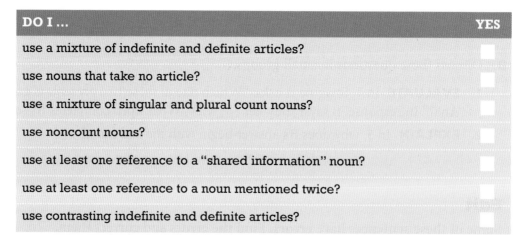

DO I ...	YES
use a mixture of indefinite and definite articles?	☐
use nouns that take no article?	☐
use a mixture of singular and plural count nouns?	☐
use noncount nouns?	☐
use at least one reference to a "shared information" noun?	☐
use at least one reference to a noun mentioned twice?	☐
use contrasting indefinite and definite articles?	☐

4. **PEER REVIEW** Work with a partner to help you decide how to fix your errors and improve the content.

5. **REWRITE YOUR DRAFT** Using the comments from your partner, write a final draft.

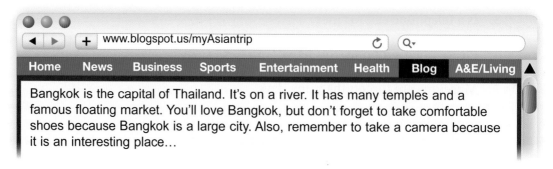

www.blogspot.us/myAsiantrip

Home | News | Business | Sports | Entertainment | Health | Blog | A&E/Living

Bangkok is the capital of Thailand. It's on a river. It has many temples and a famous floating market. You'll love Bangkok, but don't forget to take comfortable shoes because Bangkok is a large city. Also, remember to take a camera because it is an interesting place...

15

Quantity Expressions

Sustainable Communities

A1 Before You Read

Discuss these questions.

What is a sustainable community? What do you think are the goals of a sustainable community?

A2 Read

CD2 T5 Read the online article on the following page. What is a sustainable community?

A3 After You Read

Check (✓) the things that some sustainable communities have today.

✓ 1. people with shared values   _____ 5. lots of possessions

_____ 2. many residents   _____ 6. healthy lifestyles

_____ 3. places for bicycle riding   _____ 7. fast food restaurants

_____ 4. vegetable gardens   _____ 8. many cars

Tamera — A Sustainable Community

Why Is Tamera a Sustainable Community?

Tamera is a sustainable community in Portugal. Like a lot of other sustainable communities, Tamera is a place where people live together in a simple way. Some residents of Tamera moved there because they decided that living in a big city did not make them happy. They didn't like the fast pace of life, the noise, and the unhealthy conditions of a big city, so they came to live with other people who share the same values.

What Size Are Sustainable Communities?

Tamera is not large; there are only around 200 people living there. A few sustainable communities have only about 50–100 people. Other ones may have 2,000 residents, but that's still small. Small communities make healthy living possible. There isn't any noise or pollution, but there are a lot of opportunities for healthy, happy living.

What Do People Do in Sustainable Communities?

People who live in these communities only need to earn a little money, because they don't want or need a lot of stuff. Many residents work from home or in the community. Most people walk or use bicycles to get to work, so there isn't much traffic. Of course you'll see a few cars in Tamera, but people use them only if necessary. There is always some work to be done because the people of Tamera grow their own fruits and vegetables.

---

pollution: the state of being dirty and unhealthy; also, substances that cause this

resident: a person who lives in a place

sustainable: able to maintain without long-term damage to the environment

value: (often plural) an idea or belief that someone thinks is important in life

B FORM

Quantity Expressions

Think Critically About Form

A. Look back at the article on page 233 and complete the tasks below.

1. **IDENTIFY** Look at the underlined phrases. Each phrase contains a quantity expression and a noun. Circle the noun in each phrase.

2. **CATEGORIZE** Which quantity expressions go with plural count nouns? Which quantity expressions go with noncount nouns? Look at the quantity expressions below. Check (✓) the correct columns in the chart below.

QUANTITY EXPRESSIONS	PLURAL COUNT NOUNS	NONCOUNT NOUNS
a lot of		
some		
a few		
a little		
many		
much		

B. Discuss your answers with the class and read the Form charts to check them.

ONLINE PRACTICE

AFFIRMATIVE STATEMENTS		
	QUANTITY EXPRESSION	**PLURAL COUNT NOUN**
The town has	**a lot of** **many** **some** **a few** **no**	bicycles.

NEGATIVE STATEMENTS		
	QUANTITY EXPRESSION	**PLURAL COUNT NOUN**
It doesn't have	**a lot of** **many** **any**	residents.

	QUANTITY EXPRESSION	**NONCOUNT NOUN**
The town has	**a lot of** **some** **a little** **no**	work.

	QUANTITY EXPRESSION	**NONCOUNT NOUN**
It doesn't have	**a lot of** **much** **any**	traffic.

- Quantity expressions can come before plural count nouns and noncount nouns.
- Some quantity expressions are used with both plural count nouns and noncount nouns. Some are used only with plural count nouns or only with noncount nouns.

With Plural Count Nouns or Noncount Nouns	With Plural Count Nouns	With Noncount Nouns
a lot of	many	much
some	a few	a little
any		
no		

- Use *no* with the affirmative form of a verb. Use *any* with the negative form of a verb.

YES/NO QUESTIONS		
	QUANTITY EXPRESSION	PLURAL COUNT NOUN
Does the town have	**a lot of many any**	residents?

	QUANTITY EXPRESSION	NONCOUNT NOUN
Does the town have	**a lot of much any**	traffic?

INFORMATION QUESTIONS WITH *HOW MANY* AND *HOW MUCH*		
HOW MANY	PLURAL COUNT NOUN	
How many	residents	does the town have?

HOW MUCH	NONCOUNT NOUN	
How much	traffic	does the town have?

- *Much, many, a lot of,* and *any* are common in *Yes/No* questions. We sometimes use *a few, a little,* and *some,* but they are less common.
- It is not necessary to repeat the noun in the answer to questions with quantity phrases.

   A: Do you want **some** coffee?   A: **How much** traffic does the town have?

   B: Yes, I want **some**.   B: **A little**.

- *A lot of* shortens to *a lot* when we use it without a noun.

   A: Does Texas have any oil?

   B: Yes, **a lot**.

B1 Listening for Form

CD2 T6 Listen to each sentence. Write the quantity expression you hear.

1. __*Some*_____ people don't like this neighborhood, but I love it.

2. It's very quiet. We have almost _____ traffic.

3. _____ families with small children live here.

4. We don't have _____ cafés or art galleries.

5. However, we have _____ ethnic restaurants.

6. The city park is _____ blocks away.

B2 Replacing *A Lot Of* with *Much* and *Many*

Rewrite the paragraph. Replace *a lot of* with *much* or *many*.

People from a lot of different countries live in my neighborhood. On the street you hear a lot of languages. People here don't have a lot of money, but they are very friendly. For example, Mr. Lee, the Chinese grocer, doesn't speak a lot of Spanish, but he always says *buenos días* to his Spanish-speaking customers. The residents also celebrate a lot of holidays. In February a lot of residents go to the Chinese New Year celebration. And no one does a lot of work on Cinco de Mayo, a Mexican holiday. Come to my neighborhood and you can experience a lot of different cultures in one afternoon.

People from many different countries live in my neighborhood...

_____

_____

_____

_____

_____

B3 Working on Quantity Expressions

Complete each sentence. Choose the correct quantity expression in parentheses.

(A little / (Many)) sustainable communities don't have (some / any) cars. Of course,
₁ ... ₂

course, sustainable communities have (no / any) freeways, but (some / any) sustainable
₃ ... ₄

communities have (much / a lot of) bicycles.
₅

Sustainable communities don't usually have (no / any) fast food restaurants or
₆

convenience stores. They don't have (some / many) problems either. For example, they
₇

don't have (much / a little) crime and generally they have (a few / no) criminals. This is
₈ ... ₉

an advantage because they don't need (a lot of / some) police officers either. In addition,
₁₀

there isn't (much / some) noise in a sustainable community, so it's a great place to live.
₁₁

B4 Working on *A Few* and *A Little*

Complete the conversations. Use *a few* or *a little*.

Situation 1

Elena: Excuse me, Mr. Reed. I need ___a little___ help with my homework.
₁

Do you have _____ time for _____ questions?
₂ ... ₃

Mr. Reed: Of course. I have _____ minutes before my next class. What's the
₄

problem?

Elena: Well, I missed _____ classes, and I'm having _____ trouble with
₅ ... ₆

these verbs.

Situation 2

Rosa: Hi, Jack. How was Japan?

Jack: Good, but we only had _____ days there so we didn't see everything.
₁

We had _____ time in Tokyo, so we visited _____ museums.
₂ ... ₃

We did _____ shopping, too. It was great fun!
₄

B5 Forming *Yes/No* Questions with Quantity Expressions

A. Form *Yes/No* questions with quantity expressions. Use the words and phrases. Punctuate your sentences correctly.

1. a lot of/this area/have/sustainable communities/does

    Does this area have a lot of sustainable communities?

2. sustainable communities/much/have/do/crime

_____

3. a sustainable community/many/does/have/fast food stores

_____

4. do/a lot of/in/a sustainable community/telecommute/people

_____

5. sustainable communities/live/many/people/do/in

_____

6. sustainable communities/much/do/have/traffic

_____

7. do/some/a lot of/bike paths/have/sustainable communities

_____

8. residents/this sustainable community/have/does/a lot of

_____

B. Look back at the questions in part A. Choose the correct answer for each question. Both answers may be possible.

1. **a.** Yes, it does.

    b. Yes, many.

2. **a.** No, not many.

    b. No, not much.

3. **a.** No, not many.

    b. No, not much.

4. **a.** Yes, they do.

    b. Yes, a lot.

5. **a.** No, not many.

    b. No they don't.

6. **a.** No, not a lot.

    b. No, not many.

7. **a.** Yes, they do.

    b. Yes, many.

8. **a.** No, they don't.

    b. No, it doesn't.

B6 Asking Questions with *How Much* or *How Many*

A. Luisa wants to buy a house. Complete her questions to the real estate agent. Use *how much* or *how many*.

1. How many _____ rooms does the house have?

2. _____ years did the last owners live here?

3. _____ work does the house need?

4. _____ noise does the area get from the airport?

5. _____ schools are in the neighborhood?

6. _____ crime does the neighborhood have?

7. _____ people live next door?

8. _____ space does the backyard have?

B. Imagine you are the home buyer in the picture. Think of four more questions for the real estate agent. Use the words below and *how much* or *how many*.

bedrooms   public transportation   stores   traffic

How many bedrooms does the house have?

Quantity Expressions

Think Critically About Meaning and Use

A. Read the sentences and answer the questions below.

a. Phoenix has many residents. It has a lot of traffic.
b. Mineral Springs has a few residents. It has a little traffic.
c. Coalville has no residents. It has no traffic.
d. Tempe has a lot of residents. It doesn't have much traffic.

1. **IDENTIFY** Underline the quantity expressions in the sentences.

2. **EVALUATE** Which expressions refer to large numbers or amounts? Which expressions refer to small numbers or amounts?

3. **ANALYZE** Which expression means none?

B. Discuss your answers with the class and read the Meaning and Use Notes to check them.

Meaning and Use Notes

ONLINE
PRACTICE

Expressing General Quantities

▶ **1** Some quantity expressions refer to a general amount of something. They do not refer to exact amounts.

Large Quantities	• many, much, a lot of	A city has **many** residents.
↕	• some	He has **some** money.
	• a few, a little	The town has **a few** residents.
Small Quantities	• no	The town has **no** water.

Large Quantities

▶ **2A** Use *much*, *many*, and *a lot of* for large amounts. *A lot of* is more common. (Remember, we usually don't use *much* in affirmative statements.)

Plural Count Nouns	**Noncount Nouns**
Many tourists visit the town.	He has **a lot of** time.
The town has **a lot of** residents.	She doesn't have **much** money.
	Does she have **a lot of** money?

▶ **2B** In informal speech, we often use *lots of* instead of *a lot of.*

He has **lots of** time.

Lots of tourists visit the town.

Small Quantities

▶ **3** Use *a few* and *a little* for small amounts. *Some* can express a slightly greater amount.

Plural Count Nouns	**Noncount Nouns**
A few people live in Mineral Springs.	He has **a little** money.
Some people live in Mineral Springs.	He has **some** money.

Note

▶ **4** Use *no* + noun with an affirmative verb or *any* + noun with a negative verb to express none at all.

The town has **no** water. = The town does**n't have any** water.

The town has **no** residents. = The town does**n't have any** residents.

C1 Listening for Meaning and Use

▶ Notes 1–4

CD2 T7   Look at the chart. Listen to the information. How much of each thing does the speaker mention? Check (✓) the correct column.

		LARGE QUANTITIES	SMALL QUANTITIES	NONE
1.	food stores	✓		
2.	Italian food			
3.	years			
4.	money			
5.	money			
6.	people			
7.	kinds			
8.	celebrities			

C2 Expressing Opinions with Quantity Expressions ▶ Notes 1–4

Complete each statement. Use a quantity expression + noun. Use a variety of different quantity expressions. Then compare your answers with your class.

1. Young children need _a lot of love_____.

2. The students in our class have _____.

3. Good teachers have _____.

4. Students often buy _____.

5. Our school needs _____.

6. Writers need _____.

7. Most people don't want _____.

8. My neighborhood doesn't have _____.

C3 Asking and Answering Questions about Quantity ▶ Notes 1–4

A. Complete each question. Use *any, a lot of, much,* or *many.* Use each quantity expression twice. More than one answer is possible.

1. Do you have _____many_____ relatives in other countries?

2. Do you have _____ free time?

3. Do you get _____ exercise?

4. Do you eat _____ fruits and vegetables?

5. Do you need _____ sleep?

6. Do you drink _____ coffee?

7. Do your teachers give you _____ homework?

8. Do you listen to _____ music?

B. Work with a partner. Take turns asking and answering the questions in part A. Use quantity expressions in your answers.

A: Do you have many relatives in other countries?

B: No, I don't have any relatives in other countries. My relatives live in this country.

C4 Comparing Cities and Small Towns

▶ Notes 1–4

Work with a partner. Look at the pictures and think about life in big cities and small towns. List three advantages and three disadvantages of each. Use quantity expressions. Write affirmative and negative statements. Punctuate your sentences correctly.

BIG CITIES	SMALL TOWNS
Advantages	*Advantages*
Big cities have a lot of movie theaters.	
Disadvantages	*Disadvantages*
Big cities have a lot of traffic.	

Life in a big city

Life in a small town

C5 Answering a Survey with Quantity Expressions ▶ Notes 1–4

Complete this website survey. Then discuss your answers with a partner.

How Much Effort Are You Making to Improve Your English?

1

How often do you study outside of class?

_____ a. Every day. _____ b. A few days a week. _____ c. Never.

2

Do you speak any English outside of class?

_____ a. Yes, a lot. _____ b. Yes, some. _____ c. No, none.

3

Do you have many English-speaking friends?

_____ a. Yes, a lot. _____ b. No, only a few. _____ c. No, none.

4

Do you listen to many English-language radio programs?

_____ a. Yes, a lot. _____ b. Yes, some. _____ c. No, none.

5

How many songs do you know in English?

_____ a. A lot. _____ b. A few. _____ c. None.

6

Did you read any English-language novels last month?

_____ a. Yes, two or three. _____ b. Yes, one. _____ c. No, none.

7

How many English-language newspaper articles did you read last week?

_____ a. A lot. _____ b. A few. _____ c. None.

8

How often do you use an English-language dictionary?

_____ a. Every day. _____ b. A few times a week. _____ c. Never.

?

Scoring: Give yourself 2 points for every *a*, 1 point for every *b*, and 0 points for every *c*.

13-16 You are making a lot of effort. Keep up the great work!

9-12 You are making good effort. Well done!

5-8 You are making some effort.

0-4 You are not making much effort. Look at the survey for some ideas.

WRITING

Write About the Good Qualities of Your School

Think Critically About Meaning and Use

A. Complete each conversation.

1. A: Does your neighborhood have much traffic?

B: Yes, _____

    ⓐ it has a lot.

    b. it has little.

    c. it has many.

2. A: Do you want more coffee?

B: _____

    a. Yes. Just a little, please.

    b. No. Only a few, please.

    c. Yes. Just a few, please.

3. A: How much work did you do?

B: _____

    a. Many.

    b. Much.

    c. A lot.

4. A: _____

B: I only need a little.

    a. We don't have many carrots.

    b. We don't have much sugar.

    c. We have no eggs.

B. Discuss these questions in small groups.

1. **CATEGORIZE** In 1-4, which refer to large quantities? Which refer to small quantities?

2. **GENERATE** Create one sentence that refers to a large quantity and one sentence that refers to a small quantity.

Edit

Find the errors in this paragraph and correct them.

    As a first-year university student, I had ~~much~~ *many* problems. I didn't have no friends and I was very lonely. I also didn't speak a lot English then, so I had a few trouble communicating. At the beginning lot of things were strange, like the food and the subways. Luckily, I met a little students from my country, and they helped me. Today I know much people. I also speak more English, so now I don't have any problems.

Write

Write an email to your friend to tell him or her all about your school and why it would be a good idea to study there. Use quantity expressions.

1. **BRAINSTORM** List all of the good qualities of your school. Use these questions to help you.

   - What degree programs are at your school?
   - What interesting courses can you take?
   - How many students are there?
   - Are there any foreign students?
   - Which countries are they from?
   - What cultural events are there?
   - What sporting events are there?

2. **WRITE A FIRST DRAFT** Before you write your first draft, read the checklist below. Write your draft using quantity expressions.

3. **EDIT** Read your work and check it against the checklist below. Circle grammar, spelling, and punctuation errors.

DO I ...	YES
use both affirmative and negative statements with quantity expressions?	☐
use quantity expressions with both plural count nouns and noncount nouns?	☐
ask and answer *yes/no* questions with quantity expressions?	☐
ask and answer information questions with quantity expressions?	☐
use expressions for general quantities?	☐
use expressions for large quantities?	☐
use expressions for small quantities?	☐

4. **PEER REVIEW** Work with a partner to help you decide how to fix your errors and improve the content.

5. **REWRITE YOUR DRAFT** Using the comments from your partner, write a final draft.

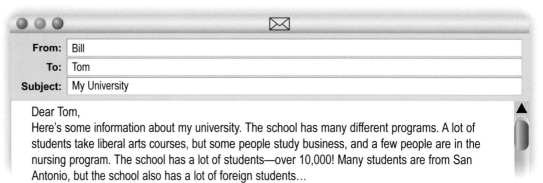

From: Bill
To: Tom
Subject: My University

Dear Tom,
Here's some information about my university. The school has many different programs. A lot of students take liberal arts courses, but some people study business, and a few people are in the nursing program. The school has a lot of students—over 10,000! Many students are from San Antonio, but the school also has a lot of foreign students…

16

There Is and *There Are*

A Wonderful Gift

A1 Before You Read

Discuss these questions.

Is there an art museum in your area? Do you like art? What kind of art is your favorite? Why?

A2 Read

CD2 T8 Read this web news article about a piece of art. Then read the two online comments on the following page. What are the writers' opinions about the piece of art?

Art News

A View from Lowell, by Mitch Jacoby

Lowell Public Library Gets Valuable Painting

FEBRUARY 2—There is a new painting by artist Mitch Jacoby at the Lowell Public Library. Mr. David Grady, president of Grady 5 Industries, recently donated the work to the library. Experts say that the painting, *A View from Lowell*, is worth half a million dollars. Local 10 art critic Melissa Sawyer said, "We are very lucky. There's no other painting like this in the whole state." Mayor Frank Kurty said that the town will pay for a new security 15 system for the painting. "There isn't enough security in the library for such a valuable piece of art."

FEBRUARY 7

Dear Editor:

I went to the library yesterday to see *A View from Lowell*. It's ridiculous!
There are houses and gardens in Lowell. There are no houses and gardens in
20 this painting. There are stores in Lowell. There aren't any stores in this painting
either. What is there in this painting? Well, it's all gray! There are dark gray
squares and light gray rectangles. There's a gray circle in the middle. Is this
Lowell? No way! Is this art? Absolutely not. It's a geometry lesson!
Experts say that this painting is worth half a million dollars. Let's sell it and buy
25 a real piece of art.

DR. ARTHUR MONTGOMERY, Lowell

FEBRUARY 16

Dear Editor:

A recent letter to the editor was very critical of Mitch Jacoby's painting, *A View
from Lowell*. Local doctor Arthur Montgomery does not believe that this painting
30 is art. Of course, there are always many different opinions about art. Dr.
Montgomery has a right to his opinion, but no one is telling him to hang this
painting in his home. Frankly, when I have a health problem, I'll ask Dr.
Montgomery's opinion. About art, I'll trust the experts.

SUSAN CALDWELL, Lowell

---

art critic: a person who gives professional opinions
about art

critical: saying what is wrong with somebody or
something

expert: a person who knows a lot about a subject

valuable: worth a lot of money

A3 After You Read

Write *T* for true or *F* for false for each statement.

_F_ **1.** The library doesn't need a security system.

_____ **2.** The painting, *A View from Lowell*, is now worth a million dollars.

_____ **3.** There is no local art critic in Lowell.

_____ **4.** There are many paintings like it in the state.

_____ **5.** Dr. Montgomery is an art expert.

_____ **6.** The painting is very colorful.

B FORM

There Is and *There Are*

Think Critically About Form

A. Look back at the article and the two letters on pages 248–249 and complete the tasks below.

1. **IDENTIFY** Look at the underlined examples of *there is* and *there are*. Circle the noun or noun phrase that follows each example.

2. **ANALYZE** Which form of *there is/there are* comes before a singular noun? Which form comes before a plural noun?

3. **RECOGNIZE** Find more examples of *there is* and *there are*.

B. Discuss your answers with the class and read the Form charts to check them.

 ONLINE PRACTICE

SINGULAR AFFIRMATIVE STATEMENTS		
THERE + IS	NOUN PHRASE	
There is **There's**	a library a lot of traffic	in town.

PLURAL AFFIRMATIVE STATEMENTS		
THERE	*ARE*	NOUN PHRASE	
There	**are**	two libraries a lot of cars	in town.

SINGULAR NEGATIVE STATEMENTS		
THERE	*IS + NOT*	NOUN PHRASE	
There	**is not** **isn't**	a museum much traffic	in town.

PLURAL NEGATIVE STATEMENTS		
THERE	*ARE + NOT*	NOUN PHRASE	
There	**are not** **aren't**	any museums many cars	in town.

YES/NO QUESTIONS		
IS/ARE	*THERE*	NOUN PHRASE	
Is	**there**	a museum any traffic	in town?
Are		any banks	

SHORT ANSWERS					
YES	THERE	IS/ARE	NO	THERE	IS/ARE + NOT
Yes,	**there**	**is.**	No,	**there**	**isn't.**
		are.			**aren't.**

QUESTIONS ABOUT QUANTITY WITH *HOW MUCH* AND *HOW MANY*				
HOW MUCH/HOW MANY	**NOUN**	**IS/ARE**	**THERE**	
How much	traffic	**is**	**there**	in town?
How many	schools	**are**		

- In a statement, a noun follows *there is* and *there are*. Use *there is* with a singular count noun or a noncount noun. Use *there are* with a plural noun.
- We use an indefinite article *(a, an)* before a singular count noun in sentences with *there is*.

    There is **a** red car in the driveway.

- We often use *some* or another quantity expression before plural nouns in sentences with *there are*.

    There are **some** new shops in town.   There are **a lot of** new shops in town.

- In spoken English, we usually use *there isn't* or *there aren't* in negative statements. *There is not* and *there are not* are uncommon.
- Use *no* in affirmative statements to express the same idea as *not any* or *not a/an* + noun.

    There is **no** traffic. = There is **not any** traffic.

    There are **no** museums in town. = There are **not any** museums in town.

    There is **no** bookstore in town. = There **isn't a** bookstore in town.

> Do not use *no* and *not* in the same sentence.
>
> **X** There are not no gardens in the painting. (incorrect)

- Use *any* in questions with plural count nouns and noncount nouns.

    Are there **any** libraries in town?   Is there **any** traffic in your area?

- With *how much* and *how many*, the noun comes before *is/are* + *there*.

B1 Listening for Form

CD2 T9   Listen to the description of a new apartment. Choose the words you hear.

1. **a.** there's
   b. there are

2. **a.** there are
   b. there aren't

3. **a.** there's
   b. there are

4. **a.** there's no
   b. there isn't

5. **a.** there's
   b. there isn't

6. **a.** there isn't
   b. there aren't

B2 Writing Negative Statements with *There Is/There Are*

Change each affirmative sentence to a negative sentence. Write each negative sentence in two ways. Punctuate your sentences correctly.

1. There's traffic in my neighborhood.

   There isn't any traffic in my neighborhood.

   There's no traffic in my neighborhood.

2. There are some stores on this street.

   _____

   _____

3. There is a hospital in our town.

   _____

   _____

4. There is some crime in that neighborhood.

   _____

   _____

5. There are some children in the park.

   _____

   _____

6. There is a jewelry store at the mall.

   _____

   _____

7. There is a bus stop on my street.

   _____

   _____

8. There are some noisy people in this neighborhood.

   _____

   _____

B3 Working on *There Is/There Are*

Work with a partner. Look at the pictures. How are they different? Discuss each item below.

1. stoplight

   There is a stoplight in picture B.
   There are no stoplights in picture A.

2. supermarket

3. stop sign

4. movie theater

5. drugstore

6. children

7. bakery

B4 Writing *Yes/No* and Information Questions with *There Is/There Are*

Read each answer. Write a *Yes/No* or an information question for each answer.

1. **A:** Is there a gas station on Maple Street?

   B: No, there isn't. There isn't a gas station on Maple Street.

2. **A:** _____

   B: Yes, there are. There are some public telephones in the library.

3. **A:** _____

   B: There are 200 students at this school.

4. **A:** _____

   B: No, there isn't. There isn't a bank on Green Street.

5. **A:** _____

   B: Yes, there are. There are some expensive hotels downtown.

6. **A:** _____

   B: There are two hours of homework every night.

B5 Writing Statements and Questions with *There Is/There Are*

A. Write affirmative or negative statements with *there is* or *there are* in your notebook.

1. a good bookstore in this area

   There is a good bookstore in this area.

2. a lot of children in my neighborhood

3. interesting shows on TV tonight

4. a good article in the newspaper today

 B. Work with a partner. Ask and answer questions with *there is/there are* about the information in part A.

A: *Is there a good bookstore in this area?*

B: *Yes, there is. There is a good bookstore on the corner of Clara Avenue and Duck Street.*

MEANING AND USE

There Is and *There Are*

Think Critically About Meaning and Use

A. Read the sentences and answer the questions below.

a. "Dr. Jones, there's a patient on the telephone. He's very upset."

b. "Dr. Jones, the patient is on the telephone again. He's very upset."

1. **EVALUATE** Which sentence talks about the patient for the first time? How do you know?

2. **INTERPRET** In which sentence does the doctor already know about the patient? How do you know?

B. Discuss your answers with the class and read the Meaning and Use Notes to check them.

Meaning and Use Notes

ONLINE PRACTICE

Introducing a Noun

▶ **1** We use *there is/there are* with *a/an*, no article, or a quantity expression to talk about someone or something for the first time. After we introduce someone or something, we use *the* + noun, or a pronoun to mention that person or thing again.

Introducing a Noun	**Mentioning the Noun Again**
There's <u>a</u> drugstore on my street.	<u>The</u> drugstore is next to the bakery.
There are <u>a lot of</u> students in the class.	<u>They</u> are from different countries.

Expressing Existence, Location, and Facts

▶ **2** Sentences with *there is/there are* describe the location or the existence of someone or something, and usually state factual information.

Location	**Fact**
There's a man at the door.	**There are** 365 days in a year.

Existence

Guess what! **There's** a new Dan Brown novel.

(Continued on page 256)

> ❗ Do not confuse *there is/there are* with the adverb *there*. We use the adverb *there* when we are pointing to someone or something to tell its location.
>
> **There Is/There Are**
>
> **There's** a sweater on the bed.
>
> **There are** two blankets in the closet.
>
> **There (Adverb)**
>
> **There** is my red sweater! I left it on the bed.
>
> **There** are the blankets! I put them in the closet.
>
> Do not confuse *there is/there are* with the possessive adjective *their*. We use *their* to express ownership or possession of something.
>
> **There Is/There Are**
>
> **There's** a car in the driveway.
>
> **Their (Possessive Adjective)**
>
> **Their** car is in the driveway.

C1 Listening for Meaning and Use

▶ Notes 1, 2

 CD2 T10 Listen to each sentence. Does it introduce a noun, express possession, or point to a noun? Check (✓) the correct column.

	INTRODUCES A NOUN (THERE IS/THERE ARE)	EXPRESSES POSSESSION (THEIR)	POINTS TO A NOUN (ADVERB THERE)
1.		✓	
2.			
3.			
4.			
5.			
6.			

C2 Writing Facts

▶ Note 2

Write factual statements with *there is/there are* about each phrase in your notebook. Punctuate your sentences correctly.

1. days in a year

   There are 365 days in a year.

2. months with 28 days

3. hours in a day

4. planets in the solar system

5. sunrises every day

6. full moons every month

7. weeks in a month

8. countries in the world

C3 Describing a Picture

▶ Notes 1, 2

Work with a partner. Describe one of the pictures in each pair. Ask your partner to guess which picture you are describing.

There is a path in this picture. There are…

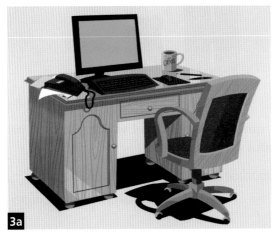

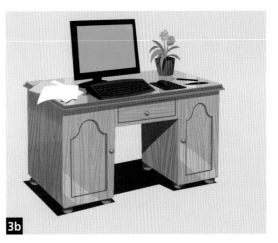

C4 Describing a Neighborhood

▶ Notes 1, 2

A. Look at the map of a neighborhood. Choose five of the places below and draw them on the map.

bank	gas station	hospital	hotel	library
museum	park	police station	post office	supermarket

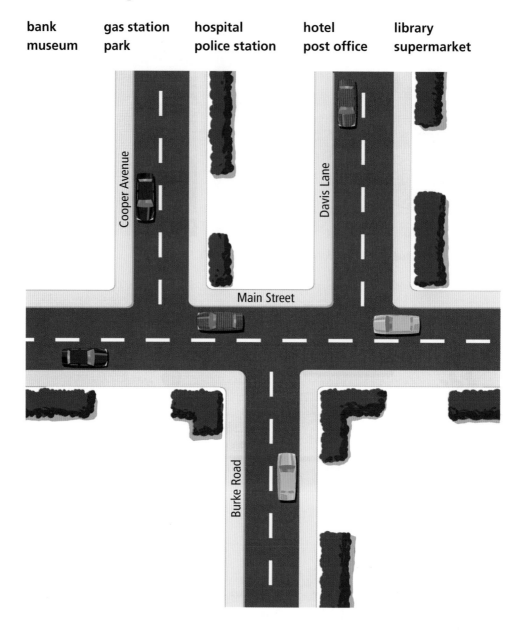

B. Now work with a partner. Ask questions to find out which places in part A are in your partner's neighborhood and where they are.

A: *Is there a bank in your neighborhood?*   A: *Is it on Burke Road?*

B: *Yes, there is.*   B: *No, it isn't. It's on Cooper Avenue.*

Beyond the Sentence

Combining Sentences with *But*

But can be used to combine sentences with contrasting information. Often the information is surprising. Use a comma when combining two complete sentences with *but*.

> There's a plate on the table. There's no food on the plate.
>
> There's a plate on the table, **but** there's no food on it.

When we write, we combine sentences because it makes our writing sound more natural. Compare these two paragraphs.

A.

There isn't much to do in our town. There are a lot of supermarkets. There aren't any movie theaters. We have three gas stations. We don't have any good restaurants. The young people have plenty of time. They don't have any after-school activities. They have money. There are no shops.

B.

There isn't much to do in our town. There are a lot of supermarkets, but there are no movie theaters. We have three gas stations, but we don't have any good restaurants. The young people have plenty of time, but they don't have any after-school activities. They have money, but there are no shops.

C5 Combining Sentences with *But*

Rewrite the paragraph below. Use *but* to combine the underlined sentences. Punctuate your sentences correctly.

There's a new student in our class. <u>Her first name is Ana. I don't know her last name.</u> <u>Her English seems pretty good. She never says much in class.</u> She's from South America. <u>There are four students in my class from Venezuela. Ana is the only one from Argentina.</u>

_____

_____

_____

_____

_____

WRITING   Write About Your Neighborhood

 Think Critically About Meaning and Use

A. Complete each conversation.

1. A: Is there a drugstore in your neighborhood?

B: _____

   a. No, it isn't.

   (b.) No, there isn't.

   c. Yes, they are.

2. A: Put the books on the table, please.

B: _____

   a. There isn't any room.

   b. There's the table.

   c. No, there isn't.

3. A: _____

B: No, there isn't.

   a. How many hotels are there in your hometown?

   b. Is there a hotel in your hometown?

   c. Are there many hotels in your hometown?

4. A: Are there any children in your house?

B: _____

   a. Yes, they are.

   b. No, there isn't.

   c. Yes, there are two.

5. A: Is the book on the desk?

B: _____

   a. No, it isn't.

   b. Yes, there is.

   c. Yes, there are.

6. A: _____

B: Yes, there is.

   a. Is their car in the driveway?

   b. Are there cars in the driveway?

   c. Is there a car in the driveway?

B. Discuss these questions in small groups.

1. PREDICT In 4, imagine that no children live in B's house. How does B answer A's question?

2. EVALUATE Imagine that A asks, "Is their car in the driveway?" In the response, B says, "No, _____ isn't." What word completes B's sentence?

Edit

Some of these sentences have errors. Find the errors and correct them.

1. There is *are* three boys here.

2. Is their car at the mechanic's?

3. Is there any oranges in the kitchen?

4. Are there any English class in the morning?

5. Is there a telephone message for me?

6. There are no children at school today.

7. There are some book here.

8. There aren't no chairs.

9. There are any students in the hall?

10. Look in the refrigerator. Are there any sandwich?

Write

Write a paragraph about your neighborhood. Use *there is* and *there are*.

1. **BRAINSTORM** Think of all the features of your neighborhood, both good and bad. Use these questions to make notes.
   - What are the good things about your neighborhood?
   - What are the bad things about your neighborhood?
   - What kinds of stores are there?
   - How is the traffic?
   - What kinds of jobs are there?
   - Are there any parks?
   - What kind of entertainment is there?
   - What are the other services (e.g., banks, gas stations, etc.)?

2. **WRITE A FIRST DRAFT** Before you write your first draft, read the checklist below. Look at the examples on page 259 and write your draft using *There is* and *There are*.

3. **EDIT** Read your work and check it against the checklist below. Circle grammar, spelling, and punctuation errors.

DO I...	YES
make affirmative and negative statements with *there is* and *there are*?	☐
ask and answer *yes/no* questions with *there is* and *there are*?	☐
ask and answer questions about quantity with *how much* and *how many*?	☐
use *there is* and *there are* to introduce a noun?	☐
use *there is* and *there are* to express existence, location, and facts?	☐
use *their* and *there* at least once each in the entry?	☐
use *but* to combine sentences with contrasting information?	☐

4. **PEER REVIEW** Work with a partner to help you decide how to fix your errors and improve the content.

5. **REWRITE YOUR DRAFT** Using the comments from your partner, write a final draft.

> My neighborhood is good in many ways. There are many supermarkets, and there are a lot of nice people. They are helpful and friendly. There are also bad things about my neighborhood. For example, there aren't many restaurants, and there isn't a movie theater, but there is a big park. Is there too much traffic in my neighborhood? No, there isn't too much traffic, but it's hard to find a place to park...

Choose the correct word or words to complete each sentence.

1. Luiz isn't taking _____ classes this semester.

   a. much   **b.** some   **c.** many   **d.** a few

2. Susan speaks _____ Chinese.

   a. any   **b.** a little   **c.** a few   **d.** many

3. _____ a bus line on Maple Street?

   a. Is it   **b.** Is there   **c.** Are there   **d.** Are they

4. Listen! _____ someone at the door.

   a. There are   **b.** There's   **c.** Are there   **d.** Is it

5. We have _____ crime in our neighborhood at night.

   a. some   **b.** many   **c.** a few   **d.** any

6. My town doesn't have _____ public transportation.

   a. no   **b.** any   **c.** a few   **d.** none

7. _____ any water in the swimming pool?

   a. Are there   **b.** There is   **c.** Is there   **d.** There are

Choose the correct response to complete each conversation.

8. **A:** How much sugar do you want in your coffee?

   B: _____

   a. Just a little.   **c.** A few.

   b. Many.   **d.** Too much.

9. **A:** Our house is very small.

   B: _____

   a. Do you live in a big house?   **c.** What kind of apartment is it?

   b. How many bedrooms does it have?   **d.** Is your house big or small?

Choose *a*, *an*, or *the* to complete each sentence. Choose *X* when *a*, *an*, or *the* is <u>not</u> necessary in the sentence.

10. Luis has _____ degree in architecture.

    a. a   **b.** an   **c.** X   **d.** the

11. Ben's office is in _____ old building.

    a. a   **b.** an   **c.** X   **d.** the

12. Museums are fun on _____ rainy days.

    a. X   **b.** the   **c.** a   **d.** an

Complete each conversation with *a*, *an*, or *the*. Choose *X* when *a*, *an*, or *the* is <u>not</u> necessary in the sentence.

13. **A:** Do you have _____ hammer?
    B: No, why do you need one?

14. **A:** Meet me in _____ hour in the parking lot.
    B: Sure. No problem.

15. **A:** Did you pass _____ math exam?
    B: Yes, I got an A.

16. **A:** What time do you want to leave?
    B: At 8:00. _____ show starts at 8:45.

Match the response to the question below.

17. Where is my shirt?

18. How much milk is there?

19. Is there a lot of traffic on your street?

20. Is there a full moon tonight?

    a. There are exactly 100.

    b. There's about a quart.

    c. It's there, on the chair.

    d. No, there isn't. It's very quiet.

    e. Yes, there is. It's very bright.

    f. Their home is across the street.

The Future with *Be Going To*

A GRAMMAR IN DISCOURSE

Sports News Now

A1 Before You Read

Discuss these questions.

Do you read magazines? What kind of magazines do you like? Why?

A2 Read

 CD2 T11 Read this page from the table of contents of a magazine. What sports teams does the magazine talk about?

▶▶▶ *Sports News Now*

BASEBALL   **page 22**

The New Jersey Diamonds are going to play for their second championship this season. Are they going to win? What do the fans think? Alex Cortes has the predictions.

• *"The Diamonds aren't going to win it again this year. They were lucky last year,*
5 *and they were lucky this year. That luck is going to end soon."*
Larry Markle, mechanic, Patterson

• *"The Diamonds are probably going to do it. The team is healthy, and they have a good manager. The Sharks are probably going to*
10 *give them some trouble, but the Diamonds have a good chance."*
Amy Reed, nurse, Perth Amboy

SOCCER   **page 31**

It's official—Victor Mundsen isn't going to play for the
15 Lancaster Lions next season. What is he going to do? Is he going to retire? Carol Gray has the answers.

• *"I'm not going to lie. It was a hard decision, but it's the right decision. I'm going to miss Lancaster, and of course, all the fans."*
20 **Victor Mundsen**

Women's basketball is the hot sport this year, and the Miami Twisters are the hot team. But just last week, the Twisters' star player, Marta Sanchez, announced
25 her retirement. Who is going to emerge as the new star of the Twisters? As Sally Gordon reports, many people think Holly Jones is going to be the one.

- *"Holly is the one to watch. She's a fantastic athlete. She's going to be a top scorer."*
30 **Twisters coach, Gloria Harris**

- *"Holly is great for the team. She's young, but everyone respects her. She's going to be a terrific leader."*
Twisters center, Susan Witt

---

championship: a series of competitions to find the best player or team

coach: a person who trains people to compete in sports

emerge: to come forward

fan: a person who is very enthusiastic about a sport, movie star, etc.

top scorer: the player who scores the most points

A3 After You Read

Write *T* for true or *F* for false for each statement.

__T__ **1.** The New Jersey Diamonds won the championship last year.

_____ **2.** Amy Reed thinks The Diamonds are going to win the championship.

_____ **3.** Victor Mundsen is going to play for the Lancaster Lions next season.

_____ **4.** The Lancaster Lions are a baseball team.

_____ **5.** Marta Sanchez retired from the Twisters.

_____ **6.** Holly Jones is probably going to score a lot of points.

The Future with *Be Going To*

Think Critically About Form

A. Look back at the table of contents from the magazine on pages 266–267 and complete the tasks below.

1. ANALYZE Look at the underlined examples of the future with *be going to*. Which one is singular? Which one is plural? What verb form follows *to*?

2. SUMMARIZE Find two examples of negative forms of *be going to*. How do we form the negative of *be going to*?

B. Discuss your answers with the class and read the Form charts to check them.

ONLINE PRACTICE

AFFIRMATIVE STATEMENTS			
SUBJECT	**BE**	**GOING TO**	**BASE FORM OF VERB**
I	am		
You	are		
He She It	is	going to	help.
We			
You	are		
They			

NEGATIVE STATEMENTS				
SUBJECT	**BE**	**NOT**	**GOING TO**	**BASE FORM OF VERB**
I	am			
You	are			
He She It	is	not	going to	help.
We				
You	are			
They				

CONTRACTIONS		
I'm		
You're		
He's She's It's	going to	help.
We're		
You're		
They're		

CONTRACTIONS		
I'm not		
You're not You aren't		
He's not He isn't	going to	help.
They're not They aren't		

YES/NO QUESTIONS										

BE	SUBJECT	GOING TO	BASE FORM OF VERB
Am	I		
Are	you		
Is	he	going to	help?
	we		
Are	you		
	they		

SHORT ANSWERS					
YES	SUBJECT	BE	NO	SUBJECT + BE + NOT	
	you	are.		you **aren't.** you**'re not.**	
	I	am.		I**'m not.**	
	he	is.		he **isn't.** he**'s not.**	
Yes,	you		No,	you **aren't.** you**'re not.**	
	we	are.		we **aren't.** we**'re not.**	
	they			they **aren't.** they**'re not.**	

INFORMATION QUESTIONS						ANSWERS
WH- WORD	BE	SUBJECT	GOING TO	BASE FORM OF VERB		
How	am	I		help	Mary?	You**'re going to** pick her up.
What	are	you		cook?		Chicken.
When	is	he	going to	call	us?	Tomorrow.
Where		we		put	the sofa?	In the living room.
Who	are	you		invite?		Our friends.
Why		they		drive	to school?	Because they're late.

WH- WORD (SUBJECT)	BE		GOING TO	BASE FORM OF VERB		
Who	is		going to	call?		Karen.
What				happen?		Nothing.

! Do not use contractions with affirmative short answers.

When *who* or *what* is the subject of an information question, do not use a subject pronoun.

B1 Listening for Form

CD2 T12 Listen to the interview with Victor Mundsen, a soccer player. What form of *be going to* do you hear? Choose the correct answer.

1. **(a.)** are you going to
   b. you're going to

2. **a.** I'm not going to
   b. I'm going to

3. **a.** the fans are going to
   b. are the fans going to

4. **a.** you're going to
   b. are you going to

5. **a.** I'm going to
   b. am I going to

6. **a.** we're going to
   b. we're not going to

B2 Working on Affirmative and Negative Statements with Be Going To

A. Complete the conversations. Use the correct affirmative form of *be going to* and the verb in parentheses. Use contractions when possible.

Conversation 1

Rob: The Yankees ___are going to be___ (be) good again this year.
                                    1

Derek: And how about the Boston Red Sox? They're always good. They

_____ (have) a great year, too.
          2

Conversation 2

Tom: Our new pitcher _____ (help) us a lot. He
                                    1

_____ (give) the other teams a hard time.
          2

Yuji: The fans _____ (enjoy) this season.
                        3

Tom: I know. It _____ (be) very exciting!
                        4

B. Rewrite the sentences below in your notebook. Change the affirmative statements to negative statements. Use contractions when possible.

1. The next Summer Olympic Games are going to be in Antarctica.

   The next Summer Olympic Games aren't going to be in Antarctica.

2. People are going to live on the moon in the next ten years.

3. I am going to meet the president.

4. The population of the world is going to decrease by 2020.

5. Scientists are going to discover life on Mars.

Informally Speaking

Reduced Forms of *Going To*

CD2 T13 Look at the cartoon and listen to the conversation. How is the underlined form in the cartoon different from what you hear?

What are your plans for the weekend?

We're <u>going to</u> go to the basketball game.

We often pronounce *going to* as /gənə/ in informal speech.

Standard Form	What You Might Hear
I'm **going to** call at 8:00.	"I'm /gənə/ call at 8:00."
John is **going to** go now.	"John is /gənə/ go now."
We're **going to** eat lunch soon.	"We're /gənə/ eat lunch soon."

B3 Understanding Informal Speech

CD2 T14 Listen to the sentences. Write the standard form of the verb you hear.

1. My sister _____is going to get_____ tickets for the game this weekend.

2. All my friends _____ here.

3. They _____ me play.

4. Our team _____ tonight.

5. The Astros _____ tonight.

6. The weather _____ nice for our game this weekend.

7. Our game _____ exciting.

8. My friends and I _____ to dinner after the game.

B4 Working on *Yes/No* Questions

Write *Yes/No* questions with *be going to*. Use the phrases in parentheses. Punctuate your sentences correctly.

1. **A:** _Are you going to join a soccer league?_____ (join a soccer league)

    B: No, I'm not. I don't play soccer.

2. **A:** _____ (attend the games)

    B: Yes, we are. We go to all the games.

3. **A:** _____ (rain tomorrow)

    B: No, it isn't. The newspaper said no rain until Friday.

4. **A:** _____ (the Tigers lose)

    B: No, they aren't. They always win at home.

5. **A:** _____ (have practice tonight)

    B: Yes, we are. The coach thinks we need it.

6. **A:** _____ (win the championship)

    B: Of course we are.

B5 Forming Information Questions

Imagine you are going to interview a famous athlete. In your notebook, form information questions to ask in the interview. Use the words and phrases below. Punctuate your sentences correctly.

1. retire/when/you/going/are/to

    When are you going to retire?

2. you/are/where/going to/play/next year

3. are/why/going to/you/change teams

4. what/you/do/going to/after you retire/are

5. a championship/your team/going to/win/is/when

6. is/your new coach/who/be/going to/next season

C

The Future with *Be Going To*

Think Critically About Meaning and Use

A. Read the sentences and answer the questions below.

   a. I'm going to study in Ireland this summer. I already have my plane ticket.
   b. Be careful! Your shoe is untied. You're going to trip.

   1. ANALYZE Which sentence talks about a future plan?

   2. ANALYZE Which sentence talks about a belief about the near future?

B. Discuss your answers with the class and read the Meaning and Use Notes to check them.

Meaning and Use Notes

ONLINE PRACTICE

Expressing Future Plans

▶ **1**   Use *be going to* to talk about future plans.

   I'm going to study in Greece this summer. I got my tickets yesterday.

   We're going to study hard for the test next week. We need good grades.

Making Predictions

▶ **2**   Use *be going to* for predictions (beliefs about the future), especially when you have evidence that something is about to happen.

   Be careful! That glass **is going to fall**!

   It's cloudy. I think it**'s going to** rain soon.

Expressing Less Certain Plans and Predictions

▶ **3**   Use *probably* with *be going to* when a plan or prediction is not certain.

   A Plan

   We're probably going to get tickets for the concert, but they're very expensive.

   A Prediction

   I'm probably going to get a B, but I'm not sure.

C1 Listening for Meaning and Use

▶ Notes 1, 2

🔊 CD2 T15 Listen to the sentences. Are they plans or predictions? Check (✓) the correct column.

	PLANS	PREDICTIONS
1.		✓
2.		
3.		
4.		
5.		
6.		
7.		
8.		

C2 Talking About Future Plans

▶ Notes 1, 3

A. Write three things that you plan to do after class today. Use *be going to* + verb. Punctuate your sentences correctly.

1. _Tonight I'm going to make dinner for my friends._

2. _____

3. _____

Write three things that you plan to do this weekend. Use *be going to* + verb.

4. _____

5. _____

6. _____

Write two things that you plan to do after you complete this course. Use *be going to* + verb.

7. _____

8. _____

B. Ask several classmates about their plans.

A: *What are you going to do after class today?*

B: *I'm going to wash my car.*

Vocabulary Notes

Future Time Expressions

We use certain expressions to refer to future time. Some refer to a specific time, but others refer to general time.

Specific Time The following phrases refer to a specific time.

tomorrow   next (week/month/year/Monday)

the day after tomorrow   this (afternoon/evening/week/year)

It's going to rain **tomorrow**.

Irina is going to arrive **the day after tomorrow**.

I'm going to graduate **next year**.

She's going to cook **this afternoon**.

General Time The following phrases refer to general time.

later   soon   someday

They're going to help us **later**.

We're going to leave **soon**.

I'm going to write a book **someday**.

C3 Using Future Time Expressions

A. Write plans for the future. Use *be going to* and the future time expression in parentheses. Punctuate your sentences correctly.

1. _We're going to have a math test tomorrow morning._ (tomorrow morning)

2. _____ (next semester)

3. _____ (later)

4. _____ (next Friday)

5. _____ (the day after tomorrow)

6. _____ (someday)

B. Work with a partner. Take turns asking and answering information questions about the plans in part A. Use complete sentences as answers.

A: *When are we going to have a math test?*

B: *We're going to have a math test tomorrow morning.*

C4 Making Predictions

▶ Notes 2, 3

Look at the pictures. Make predictions about what is going to happen.

1. <u>The plane is going to land.</u>

4. _____

2. _____

5. _____

3. _____

6. _____

WRITING
Write About What a Famous Person is Going to Do in the Future

 Think Critically About Meaning and Use

A. Complete each conversation.

1. A: We're going to leave for the show at 7:00. Do you need a ride?

B: _____

   a. Sorry. I'm busy right now.
   (b.) That's great. Thanks!
   c. What time did you go?

2. A: I'm going to take biology.

B: _____

   a. Was it hard?
   b. Are you enjoying it?
   c. Who is going to teach the class?

3. A: Oh, no! Look at those black clouds!

B: _____

   a. It's probably going to rain.
   b. It rains.
   c. It rained.

4. A: Are you going to leave early?

B: Yes, _____

   a. I left at 5:00.
   b. I have an appointment at 5:00.
   c. It was 5:00.

B. Discuss these questions in small groups.

1. EVALUATE Why is *be going to* used to talk about the future in these questions?

2. COMPARE AND CONTRAST In 3, how does the meaning change if B says, "It's going to rain."?

Edit

Some of these sentences have errors. Find the errors and correct them.

1. We *are* ~~be~~ going to eat at 8:00.

2. Where are you going be tomorrow?

3. Are they going to happy?

4. They're not going to win.

5. Who is going to being your coach?

6. Carl is going to not be a great player.

Write

Write an article for an online magazine to give predictions about what you think a famous person is going to do in the future. Use the future with *be going to*.

1. **BRAINSTORM** Write down the name of the person and use the following questions to help you think about what you are going to include in your article.
   - Who is the person?
   - Why is he/she famous?
   - What is this person doing right now?
   - What are some of his/her plans or projects?
   - Is this person going to be successful? Why? or Why not?

2. **WRITE A FIRST DRAFT** Before you write your first draft, read the checklist below and look at the examples using sports teams on pages 266 and 267. Write your draft using the future with *be going to*.

3. **EDIT** Read your work and check it against the checklist below. Circle grammar, spelling, and punctuation errors.

DO I ...	YES
use the future with *be going to*?	☐
make affirmative and negative statements with *be going to*?	☐
ask and answer *Yes/No* questions?	☐
ask and answer information questions with *Wh-* question words?	☐
express future plans?	☐
make predictions?	☐
express less certain plans and predictions?	☐
use future time expressions?	☐

4. **PEER REVIEW** Work with a partner to help you decide how to fix your errors and improve the content.

5. **REWRITE YOUR DRAFT** Using the comments from your partner, write a final draft.

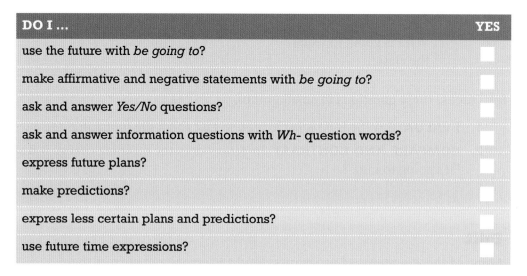

> **Jillian Wonders** is the latest celebrity to hit the ice dancing scene. She is only 14 years old, but has already won five world championships. She is going to participate in the Fifteenth Annual Ice Dancing Championship in Sweden in February, and everyone expects that she is going to win the title. What is she going to do before that event? She is probably going to practice night and day in order to win the contest...

Couch Potatoes Beware

A1 Before You Read

Discuss these questions.

Do you exercise regularly? What kind of exercise do you do?

A2 Read

CD2 T16 Read the advertisement on the following page. What product is it for? Do you think anyone will buy the product? Why or why not?

A3 After You Read

Write *T* for true or *F* for false for each statement.

___F___ **1.** A couch potato is an exercise machine.

_____ **2.** The ad says that being in shape is easy.

_____ **3.** The machine will make you slim in three days.

_____ **4.** The company will bill you in six payments.

_____ **5.** The exercise equipment costs almost $180.

_____ **6.** If you are unhappy with the machine, you'll get your money back.

Couch Potatoes BEWARE...

Winter Doesn't Last Forever!

It's wintertime. It's cold and dark. You spend a lot of time in front of the TV. You eat a lot and don't move much. In short, you're a couch potato.

5 Well, be careful! You'll be sorry in the summer! You won't be in shape. Your clothes won't fit, and you'll probably be embarrassed at the beach.

What can you do?

10 The answer is easy! Buy our **Stomach-System Exercise Equipment**, and you'll be ready for summer!

Are you afraid that exercise will be boring?

15 Don't worry! Just ten minutes a day with our magic machine and you'll be slim and fit in just a few weeks!

Call us today, and we'll send your **Stomach-System Exercise Equipment** 20 immediately! We'll bill you in six small payments of only **$29.99**. And don't worry. If you're unhappy for any reason, send the equipment back, and we'll return your money.

---

beware: be careful
couch potato: informal expression for a person who watches TV and doesn't exercise

in shape: physically fit and healthy
in short: in a few words
slim: thin

B FORM

The Future with *Will*

Think Critically About Form

A. Read the sentences and complete the task below.

    a. You will be fit in just a few weeks.

    b. We will bill you in six payments.

APPLY Look at the sentences. Underline the subject of each sentence. Does the form of *will* change or stay the same with different subjects?

B. Discuss your answers with the class and read the Form charts to check them.

ONLINE PRACTICE

AFFIRMATIVE STATEMENTS			
SUBJECT	*WILL*	BASE FORM OF VERB	
I			
You			
He She It	will	be	late.
We			
You			
They			

NEGATIVE STATEMENTS				
SUBJECT	*WILL*	*NOT*	BASE FORM OF VERB	
I				
You				
He She It	will	not	be	late.
We				
You				
They				

CONTRACTIONS		
I'll		
You'll		
He'll She'll It'll	be	late.
We'll		
You'll		
They'll		

CONTRACTIONS			
I			
You			
He She It	won't	be	late.
We			
You			
They			

YES/NO QUESTIONS			
WILL	**SUBJECT**	**BASE FORM OF VERB**	
Will	I you he she it we you they	**finish**	tomorrow?

SHORT ANSWERS						
YES	**SUBJECT**	**WILL**	**NO**	**SUBJECT**	**WILL + NOT**
Yes,	you I he she it you we they	**will**.	No,	you I he she it you we they	**won't**.

INFORMATION QUESTIONS					ANSWERS
WH- WORD	**WILL**	**SUBJECT**	**BASE FORM OF VERB**		
How	will	I	**do**	on the exam?	You**'ll** do fine.
What	will	you	**do**	now?	I**'ll** get a new job.
When	will	she	**get**	here?	Soon, I hope.
Where	will	we	**park**	the car?	We**'ll** park the car in the garage.
Who	will	you	**ask**	to the opera?	Our neighbors.
Why	will	they	**leave**	early?	They need to study.

WH- WORD (SUBJECT)	**WILL**		**BASE FORM OF VERB**		
Who	will		**win**	the game?	I don't know.
What	will		**happen**?		Nothing.

- Use the same form of *will* with every subject.
- We usually use the contracted subject pronoun + *'ll* in conversations.
- When *who* or *what* is the subject of an information question, do not use a subject pronoun.

B1 Listening for Form

CD2 T17 Listen to the conversation. Do you hear the simple present, the future with *will*, or the future with *be going to*? Check (✓) the correct column.

	SIMPLE PRESENT	FUTURE WITH *WILL*	FUTURE WITH *BE GOING TO*
1.			✓
2.			
3.			
4.			
5.			
6.			

B2 Working on Affirmative and Negative Statements with *Will*

Complete the sentences from ads. Use *will* or *won't* and the verbs in parentheses. Use contractions when possible.

1. Use Aura and your hair _____will shine_____ (shine).

2. You _____ (be) a loser in Rabino running shoes.

3. You _____ (look) like a millionaire in your new Lexia.

4. Buy a ticket on Northeastern Airlines and your friend _____ (fly) for free.

5. Take your children to Water Fun, and they _____ (forget) it.

B3 Forming Questions with *Will*

Form information questions with *will* and write them in your notebook. Use the words and phrases. Punctuate your sentences correctly.

1. get/your family/when/a new car/will

   When will your family get a new car?

2. will/when/dinner/be ready

3. where/in five years/will/be/your best friend

4. you/who/will/call

5. tomorrow/what/you/will/wear

6. how/she/home/get/will

Informally Speaking

CD2 T18

Reduced Forms of Will

Look at the cartoon and listen to the sentence. How is the underlined form in the cartoon different from what you hear?

> Don't worry. <u>Jenny will</u> be great with the kids.

In informal speech, we sometimes use the reduced form of will (*'ll*) with *wh*-words and nouns.

Standard Form	What You Might Hear
Kim **will** help you.	"/ˈkɪməl/ help you."
The weather **will** be good.	"The /ˈwɛðərəl/ be good."
When **will** he leave?	"/ˈwɛnəl/ he leave?"

B4 Understanding Informal Speech

CD2 T19

Listen to each sentence. Write the full form of the contraction with *will* that you hear.

1. Use our lotion today and your _____skin will_____ feel softer.

2. Some of my _____ believe anything.

3. Oh, no! _____ your parents say?

4. The cold _____ end tomorrow.

5. _____ be the winner? You decide! Send your vote by email.

6. Use this product and your _____ be incredibly white!

The Future with *Will*

Think Critically About Meaning and Use

A. Read the conversations and answer the questions below.

a. **Carl:** Do you want milk or soda?
   Paul: I'll have milk.

b. **Father:** You need to improve your grades.
   Son: I know. I'll work very hard this semester.

c. **Mike:** Do you think Greg will finish first?
   Steve: No, Greg won't win. Tom will.

1. ANALYZE Which conversation makes a prediction about the future?

2. ANALYZE Which conversation makes a promise?

3. DIFFERENTIATE Which conversation expresses a quick decision at the moment of speaking?

B. Discuss your answers with the class and read the Meaning and Use Notes to check them.

Meaning and Use Notes

ONLINE PRACTICE

Predictions
▶ **1A**   Use *will* to make predictions about the future.   I think the president **will solve** the problem. He always does.
▶ **1B**   Add *probably* to make the prediction less certain.   She **will probably attend** college in the fall.   I **will probably move** next year.

Promises
▶ **2**   Use *will* to express a promise, especially with *I* or *we*.   Please let me borrow your laptop. I **won't break** it.   Please let me watch this TV show. I**'ll do** my homework later.

	Quick Decisions

▶ **3** Use *will* for decisions that you make at the moment of speaking.

In a Restaurant
A: Would you like coffee or tea?
B: I'**ll have** coffee.

At Home
A: Oh, no! We're out of milk.
B: That's OK. I'**ll go** to the store.

C1 Listening for Meaning and Use

▶ Notes 1A–3

CD2 T20 Listen to each sentence. Is it a prediction, a promise, or a quick decision? Check (✓) the correct column.

	PREDICTION	PROMISE	QUICK DECISION
1.		✓	
2.			
3.			
4.			
5.			
6.			
7.			
8.			

C2 Making Promises

▶ Note 2

Read each situation. Write a promise for each one in your notebook. Use the first-person subject pronoun *I*.

1. Holly came home very late. Her father is worried. What does she say?

   I won't be late again.

2. Rob's apartment is a mess. His roommate is angry. What does Rob say?

3. Ana borrowed her friend's white dress. She spilled black coffee on it. What does Ana say to her friend?

4. Carl fell asleep in a meeting. His boss is very angry. What does Carl say to his boss?

5. Keiko washed the dishes. She is very tired. What does her husband say?

6. Ron was driving over the speed limit. A policeman stopped him. What does Ron say?

C3 Making Predictions

▶ Notes 1A, 1B

A. Read the statements about life in the twenty-first century. Then make predictions about life in the next century. Write them in your notebook.

Robots will do the housework.

	TWENTY-FIRST CENTURY
1.	Women do most of the housework.
2.	Children go to school five days a week.
3.	Most people work from nine to five.
4.	Computers are very expensive.
5.	People travel by car.
6.	Cars use gas.
7.	People eat three meals a day.
8.	People watch TV for relaxation.

 B. Work with a partner. Compare your predictions. Do you agree?

C4 Expressing Quick Decisions

▶ Note 3

 Work with a partner. Make a decision using *will* in each situation.

1. **Waiter:** I'm sorry. We don't have strawberry ice cream, only chocolate or vanilla.

   A: I'll have vanilla.

   B: I'll have chocolate.

2. **Ticket agent:** The 9:20 train is full. Tickets for the 9:50 and the 10:20 trains are available.

3. **Sales clerk:** That sweater comes in brown, blue, or red.

4. **Registrar:** There are two sections of History 101. Section A meets on Monday, and Section B meets on Wednesday.

5. **Hotel clerk:** The room on the fifth floor has a view of the mountains, and the room on the sixth floor has a view of the ocean.

6. **Receptionist:** The doctor is in tomorrow and on Thursday.

WRITING

Write About What You Will Do If Elected Class President

Think Critically About Meaning and Use

A. Complete each conversation.

1. A: I'll write to you every day.

B: _____

  (a.) Do you promise?

  b. Did you?

  c. You're writing.

2. A: Don't worry. You'll pass the test.

B: _____

  a. It's a test.

  b. I hope so.

  c. Are you?

3. A: Do you want the blue one or the red one?

B: _____

  a. I took the blue one.

  b. I take the blue one.

  c. I'll take the blue one.

4. A: The chocolate cake looks delicious. Do you want some?

B: _____

  a. I'll have a small piece.

  b. Yes, you do.

  c. It's a chocolate cake.

B. Discuss these questions in small groups.

1. EVALUATE In 2, why does speaker A use *will*?

2. EVALUATE In 3, why does speaker B use *will*?

Edit

Some of these sentences have errors. Find the errors and correct them.

1. She will ~~works~~ ^{work} late tonight.

2. Larry will be here tomorrow.

3. I'll to wait for you right here.

4. We willn't be home tonight.

5. Dinner will be ready at 6:00.

6. Who will goes to the library with her?

7. Will he at work next week?

8. They won't come not.

Write

Write a paragraph telling your classmates what you promise to do for them if you get elected as president of the class. Use the future with *will*.

1. **BRAINSTORM** List all the reasons why you want to be president and what you plan to do once you are elected. Use these questions to help you.
    - Why do you want to be president?
    - What are your promises to those who will vote for you?
    - How will things be better with you as president?
    - What will you do as president?
    - Why will you do these things?

2. **WRITE A FIRST DRAFT** Before you write your first draft, read the checklist below. Write your draft using *will*.

3. **EDIT** Read your work and check it against the checklist below. Circle grammar, spelling, and punctuation errors.

DO I ...	YES
make affirmative and negative statements with *will*?	☐
ask and answer *yes/no* questions with *will*?	☐
ask and answer information questions with *wh-* question words plus *will*?	☐
use at least two contracted forms of *will*?	☐
use *will* for predictions?	☐
use *will* for promises?	☐

4. **PEER REVIEW** Work with a partner to help you decide how to fix your errors and improve the content.

5. **REWRITE YOUR DRAFT** Using the comments from your partner, write a final draft.

> My name is Pedro Montoya. I'm running for class president.
>
> As class president, I will be a strong leader. I promise that I will
>
> work to extend library hours. I will make university life better
>
> for you. I hope you will vote for me...

Choose the correct word or words to complete each sentence.

1. What time _____ be home tonight?

   a. you going   **b.** you will   **c.** will you   **d.** are you

2. I _____ home for dinner.

   a. not be   **b.** will not   **c.** won't be   **d.** won't

3. Is it _____ tonight?

   a. not rain   **b.** going to rain   **c.** will rain   **d.** won't rain

4. He _____ us to the airport.

   a. going to take   **b.** take   **c.** will take   **d.** not going to take

5. When _____ going to quit his job?

   a. Pete's   **b.** Pete has   **c.** Pete is   **d.** is Pete

6. _____ wait for you downstairs.

   a. I'm   **b.** I am   **c.** I'll   **d.** I'm not

7. Who _____ to move to New York?

   a. are going   **b.** going   **c.** will go   **d.** is going

Choose the correct response to complete each conversation.

8. **A:** What are your plans?

   B: _____

   a. I didn't have any.   **c.** No, I'm not. Are you?

   b. I'm going to leave soon.   **d.** I already left.

9. **A:** We're going to leave for the show at 7:00. Do you need a ride?

   B: _____

   a. Sorry, I took the bus today.   **c.** What time did you go?

   b. That's great. Thanks.   **d.** What time was the show?

10. **A:** I'll write to you every day.

    B: _____

    a. Do you promise?   **c.** You're writing.

    b. Did you?   **d.** Did you write?

11. A: Do you want the blue one or the red one?

   B: _____

    a. I took the blue one.   **c.** I'll take the blue one.

    b. I take the blue one.   **d.** I'm taking the blue one.

12. A: Oh, no! It's raining. We'll get wet.

   B: _____

    a. Stay here. I'll get the car.   **c.** Don't worry. It rained last week, too.

    b. Don't worry. It will be sunny next week.   **d.** Stay here. I got the car.

13. A: Look at this ad. The play sounds interesting.

   B: _____

    a. Are you going to buy tickets?   **c.** Are you going to play?

    b. Are you going to read the ad?   **d.** Will you play?

14. A: Don't forget your umbrella today.

   B: _____

    a. It rains.   **c.** Does it rain?

    b. Did it rain?   **d.** Is it going to rain?

Match the response to the sentence below.

15. I don't have any cash.   **a.** I'll make you some lunch.

16. Gabi forgot her keys.   **b.** I won't tell him.

17. It's a secret.   **c.** I'll bring them to her.

        d. I'll go to the bank.

        e. Don't worry. I'll get a ladder.

Match the response to the sentence below.

18. Are you going to tell him?   **a.** Yes, I'm going to study all day.

19. Is the big exam on Monday?   **b.** It's going to rain tonight.

20. What's the weather report?   **c.** No, I'm going to take the bus.

        d. No, we're keeping it a secret.

        e. Yes, they're going to bed soon.

CHAPTER

19

May and *Might* for Present and Future Possibility

Optimist or Pessimist?

A1 Before You Read

Discuss these questions.

Do you usually believe good things will happen in the future? Why or why not? Do you ever worry about the future? Why or why not?

A2 Read

CD2 T21 **Read and complete this quiz from a psychology magazine. What kind of person are you?**

Quiz

Optimist or Pessimist?

Is the glass half empty or half full? If you are an optimist, you probably think the glass is half full. If you are a pessimist, you probably think the glass is half empty. Are you an optimist or a pessimist? Take this quiz and find out.

Read each pair of sentences. Choose the sentence that sounds more like you.

5   **1** **a.** "I'm really excited about the picnic. We <u>may meet</u> some interesting people."
         b. "I don't want to go to the picnic. People might not talk to me."

2 **a.** "That class is difficult, but it's interesting. You might enjoy it."
      b. "Don't take that class. It's difficult, and you might not pass."

3 **a.** "Open the envelope. It <u>may be</u> good news."
10   **b.** "Oh, no! A letter. Don't open it. It <u>might be</u> a bill."

4 **a.** "Explain the problem to your parents. They <u>may understand</u>."
      b. "Don't tell your parents. They may not listen."

5 **a.** "I'm not really qualified, but I'm going to apply anyway. I <u>might be</u> lucky."
      b. "I'm not going to apply for that job. I'll never get it."

---

15 **How many *a*'s did you choose? How many *b*'s?**

If you chose more *a*'s than *b*'s, you are an optimist. You always take chances because you believe that the future will be OK.

If you chose more *b*'s than *a*'s, you are a pessimist. You worry that bad things might happen. You ignore opportunities, and you don't like to take risks.

optimist: a person who believes good things are going to happen

pessimist: a person who believes bad things are going to happen

qualified: having the skills or knowledge that you need in order to do something

risks: possibilities that bad things might happen

A3 After You Read

Read the questions. Check (✓) the correct column.

	WHICH PERSON PROBABLY ...	OPTIMIST	PESSIMIST
1.	worries a lot?		✓
2.	thinks things will go wrong?		
3.	takes more risks?		
4.	is afraid about the future?		
5.	sees opportunities in life?		
6.	smiles more?		

B FORM

May and *Might*

Think Critically About Form

A. Look back at the quiz on pages 294–295 and complete the tasks below.

1. **APPLY** Look at the underlined examples of *may* + verb and *might* + verb. Circle the subjects. Do *may* and *might* have different forms with different subjects? What form of the verb follows *may* and *might*?

2. **SUMMARIZE** Find one negative form with *may* and one with *might*. How do we form the negative of *may* and *might*?

B. Discuss your answers with the class and read the Form charts to check them.

ONLINE PRACTICE

AFFIRMATIVE STATEMENTS			
SUBJECT	*MAY/MIGHT*	BASE FORM OF VERB	
I			
You			
He She It	**may** **might**	**finish**	today.
We			
You			
They			

NEGATIVE STATEMENTS				
SUBJECT	*MAY/ MIGHT*	*NOT*	BASE FORM OF VERB	
I				
You				
He She It	**may** **might**	**not**	**finish**	today.
We				
You				
They				

- *May* and *might* are modal verbs. Modal verbs are auxiliary verbs. We use modals to add meaning to a main verb.
- Like all modals, *may* and *might* come before the base form of the verb. They also have the same form with all subjects.
- *May* and *might* often have the same meaning. We use both for present and future possibility.
- Do not use contractions with *may* or *might*.

    x We mayn't go. (incorrect)

YES/NO QUESTIONS			
WILL	**SUBJECT**		**BASE FORM OF VERB**
Will	you		call?

BE	**SUBJECT**	**GOING TO**	**BASE FORM OF VERB**
Are	they	**going to**	call?

SHORT ANSWERS				
SUBJECT	**MAY/ MIGHT**	**SUBJECT**	**MAY/ MIGHT**	**NOT**
I	**may**. **might**.	I	**may might**	**not**.

SUBJECT	**MAY/ MIGHT**	**SUBJECT**	**MAY/ MIGHT**	**NOT**
They	**may**. **might**.	They	**may might**	**not**.

INFORMATION QUESTIONS		
WH- WORD (SUBJECT)	**MIGHT**	**BASE FORM OF VERB**
What	**might**	happen?
Who		come?

ANSWERS
He **might** not graduate.
Lynn's aunt.

- We do not usually use *may* or *might* in *Yes/No* questions about the future. We use *will* or *be going to* instead.
- We usually use *might* in information questions with *wh-* word subjects.

B1 Listening for Form

CD2 T22 Listen to the conversation. Does the speaker use *may, might,* or no modal? Check (✓) the correct column.

	MAY	*MIGHT*	**NO MODAL**
1.		✓	
2.			
3.			
4.			
5.			
6.			
7.			
8.			

B2 Forming Affirmative and Negative Statements

Form affirmative and negative statements with *may* or *might*. Use the words and phrases. Punctuate your sentences correctly.

1. give/may/the teacher/us/next week/an exam

   The teacher may give us an exam next week.

2. to Taiwan/go/we/may/next month

   _____

3. in a meeting/be/might/Claudia

   _____

4. not/he/might/the job/take

   _____

5. the governor/win/not/may/the election

   _____

6. not/they/might/any/money/have

   _____

B3 Asking and Answering Questions

Work with a partner. Take turns asking and answering the questions. Use short answers with *may (not)* or *might (not)*.

1. Is it going to rain tonight?

   It might.

2. Are you going to watch a movie tonight?

3. Will we have homework this week?

4. Are you going to eat at a restaurant tonight?

5. Are you going to relax this weekend?

6. Is your best friend going to call you tonight?

7. Who might visit you this year?

8. What might happen after class?

MEANING AND USE

Present and Future Possibility

Think Critically About Meaning and Use

A. Read the sentences and answer the questions below.

1a. He might fail the test tomorrow.   **2a.** The lights are on. They might be at home.
1b. He will fail the test.   **2b.** They're at home.

1. **CATEGORIZE** Which sentence refers to a possibility in the future? Which sentence refers to a possibility at the present time?

2. **EVALUATE** Which sentences show that the speaker is certain?

B. Discuss your answers with the class and read the Meaning and Use Notes to check them.

Meaning and Use Notes

ONLINE PRACTICE

Present and Future Possibility

▶ **1A**   Use *may* and *might* to talk about present or future possibility.

Present Possibility	**Future Possibility**
A: Where's Greg?	It feels cold. It **may snow** tonight.
B: I don't know. He **may be** in the library.	Tom didn't arrive on the ten o'clock bus. He **may come** on the next one.
A: Who's that man?	
B: He **might be** Dana's father.	

▶ **1B**   Use *may* or *might* when something is possible but not certain. If you are certain about the present, use the simple present or the present continuous. If you are certain about the future, use *will* or *be going to*.

Possible But Not Certain	**Certain**
A: Where's Emily?	A: Where's Robin?
B: I don't know. She **might be** upstairs.	B: She's in the kitchen. I just saw her.
A: We need to be in class by 9:00.	A: We need to be in the city by 8:00.
B: The bus **might not be** on time.	B: The train **will be** on time.
It's often late.	It's never late.

C1 Listening for Meaning and Use ▶ Notes 1A, 1B

CD2 T23 Listen to the conversation. Is the speaker expressing possibility or certainty? Check (✓) the correct column.

	POSSIBILITY	CERTAINTY
1.		✓
2.		
3.		
4.		
5.		
6.		
7.		
8.		

C2 Talking About Possibility and Certainty ▶ Notes 1A, 1B

Complete the telephone conversation. Use *might* or *will*.

Juan: What are your plans for the summer?

Paul: We don't know yet. We _____ might _____ visit Celia's parents in Brazil,
1

or we _____ go to Europe. Our son Ben is in Madrid for a year,
2

so we _____ visit him before he comes home. How about you?
3

Juan: Well, one thing is certain. We _____ not take an expensive
4

vacation this year! Our daughter Lisa _____ be a senior next
5

year, so we're saving money for college.

Paul: Oh, I understand! But aren't you going to go anywhere?

Juan: Well, we _____ visit my wife's sister in Georgia for a week, or we
6

_____ go on a camping trip to California.
7

Paul: That's great! Do you plan to go to Yosemite again?

Juan: We don't know yet. We _____ try somewhere new.
8

C3 Expressing Possibility and Certainty ▶ Notes 1A, 1B

Write at least two statements about each situation. Use *may, might,* or *will* to make statements that express possibility or certainty.

1. Your sister is planning an outdoor wedding in March.

   It might not be a good idea. It will still be cold. She may be sorry.

2. Your nephew is skateboarding. He's not wearing a helmet.

   _____

3. Your roommate has an exam at 10:00. It's 9:30. He's still in bed.

   _____

4. Your friend drives too fast. You're worried about him.

   _____

5. Your brother bought a lottery ticket. You want to wish him good luck.

   _____

C4 Talking About Possibility and Certainty ▶ Notes 1A, 1B

 Work with a partner. Read each situation, then have a conversation. Student A is a pessimist and Student B is an optimist. Use *may, might,* or *will.* Change roles after each conversation.

1. **A:** A neighbor invited you to a picnic. You are new in town and don't know anyone very well. Explain why you don't want to go.

   B: Give your partner three reasons for going to the picnic.

   A: I don't want to go. People might not speak to me.
   They might not like me.

   B: Of course they'll like you. You'll have a good time.
   You might make new friends.

2. **A:** You received flying lessons as a birthday present. Explain why you don't want to take the lessons.

   B: Give your partner three reasons for taking the flying lessons.

3. **A:** You want to ask your boss for a promotion. Explain why you feel nervous.

   B: Give your partner three reasons for asking for a promotion.

C5 Expressing Possibility and Certainty

▶ Notes 1A, 1B

Look at the pictures. What is going to happen in each situation? Write at least
one possibility and one certainty for each picture.

1. _He's going to fail the class._

   He might not tell his parents.

   He may take the class again.

2. _____

   _____

   _____

3. _____

   _____

   _____

4. _____

   _____

   _____

Think Critically About Meaning and Use

A. Complete each conversation.

1. A: Where is she going to stay?

   B: She's not sure. _____

   a. She'll stay with me.

   (b.) She might stay in a hotel.

   c. She may come.

2. A: _____

   B: Yes, it is. It may snow.

   a. It's really cold outside tonight.

   b. It's very warm today.

   c. What's the weather like?

3. A: I may not have time to go to the store.

   B: _____

   a. That's OK. I'll go.

   b. Please buy some milk at the store.

   c. Did you stop at the store?

4. A: The car won't start.

   B: _____

   a. It might be out of gas.

   b. The window might be broken.

   c. Will it start?

B. Discuss these questions in small groups.

1. **EVALUATE** Why is choice *a* in 1 incorrect?

2. **PREDICT** How could this example be changed so that choice *a* is the correct answer?

Edit

Some of these sentences have errors. Find the errors and correct them.

1. She m~~ayn~~'t arrive on time.   *may not*

2. We might to leave at noon.

3. Dan may sees him today.

4. I may visit them in June.

5. She might not be here right now.

6. What might happens tomorrow?

7. They might probably take the train tomorrow.

8. There is someone at the door. It may Jenna.

Write

Write a paragraph about what might or might not happen if you move to a new city. Use *may* and *might*.

1. **BRAINSTORM** List all of the things that you think will happen. Use these questions to make notes.
   - Will you be happy or sad?
   - Will you try to make new friends?
   - Will you stay at home?
   - Will you keep in touch with your old friends and co-workers?
   - Will you visit your old city?

2. **WRITE A FIRST DRAFT** Before you write your first draft, read the checklist below. Write your draft using modals.

3. **EDIT** Read your work and check it against the checklist below. Circle grammar, spelling, and punctuation errors.

DO I ...	YES
make affirmative and negative statements with *may* and *might*?	☐
ask *Yes/No* questions using *will*?	☐
answer *Yes/No* questions using *may* and *might*?	☐
ask and answer information questions using *may* and *might*?	☐
talk about present and future possibility?	☐
make statements about "possible" future events?	☐
make statements about "certain" future events?	☐

4. **PEER REVIEW** Work with a partner to help you decide how to fix your errors and improve the content.

5. **REWRITE YOUR DRAFT** Using the comments from your partner, write a final draft.

> At first I may be sad about moving because I'll miss my old friends. However, I won't stay home alone. I might join a sports club...

Can and *Could* for Present and Past Ability

The Youngest in His Class

A1 Before You Read

 Discuss these questions.

Do you know any very smart children? What are they good at? Do they have any problems?

A2 Read

 CD2 T24   Read the online magazine article about Jacob, a child prodigy, on the following page. What problems did he have as a young child? What problems does he have now?

A3 After You Read

Write *T* for true or *F* for false for each statement.

_T_ 1. Jacob goes to class with older students.

_____ 2. Jacob was reading at six months old.

_____ 3. Jacob tied his shoes at age two.

_____ 4. Jacob made friends easily.

_____ 5. Jacob plays on the college soccer team.

_____ 6. Jacob has a lot of friends in college.

An unusual college student

The Youngest in His Class
Life Is Not Always Easy for a Child Prodigy

Jacob is an unusual college student. Why? Because he is only ten years old. Why is a young boy like Jacob in college? The answer is that Jacob is a child
5 prodigy, a young genius. At the age of ten, Jacob can take undergraduate courses at the local university.

Even as a baby, Jacob was remarkable. He could speak at ten
10 months. He could read soon after his first birthday, and he could do math problems at the age of fourteen months. "The differences with other children in his kindergarten class were enormous,"
15 explains Holly Franklin, Jacob's mother. "For example, the other children could draw simple pictures, but they couldn't read or write. However, Jacob was already drawing molecules and reading
20 adult literature."

Not surprisingly, Jacob didn't make friends with other children easily. Life can be difficult for child prodigies. Parents of older children are often
25 jealous. And the other students in the school can be unfriendly or even hostile.

Child prodigies can do amazing things, but physically and emotionally they are still children. For example, at
30 age two, Jacob could talk intelligently about dinosaurs, but he couldn't tie his shoes. When he was six, he could discuss philosophy but easily cried when he was upset.

35 So how does Jacob like life as a college student? "Sometimes, it's lonely," he says. "I can't really be friends with my classmates. They're too old. And I like soccer, but I can't play on the team
40 because I'm too small. However, I can't be in a regular school because I'm too smart."

What are Jacob's plans for the future? He is going to be a doctor. "In the future,
45 I hope I can find a cure for cancer," he says. "And I hope I can have a normal life with friends and a family when people my own age grow up."

Click here for next page >

---

child prodigy: an extremely smart or talented child
enormous: very great or large
hostile: very unfriendly

jealous: upset because you want something that someone else has
kindergarten class: a class for five-year-old children

B FORM

Can and Could

Think Critically About Form

A. Look back at the article on page 307 and complete the tasks below.

1. **APPLY** Look at the underlined examples of *can* + verb and *could* + verb. Circle the subjects. Do *can* and *could* have different forms with different subjects? What form of the verb follows *can* and *could*?

2. **SUMMARIZE** Find one negative verb form with *can* and one with *could*. How do we form the negative of *can* and *could*?

B. Discuss your answers with the class and read the Form charts to check them.

▶ *Can* for Present Ability

ONLINE
PRACTICE

AFFIRMATIVE STATEMENTS			
SUBJECT	**CAN**	**BASE FORM OF VERB**	
I			
You			
He She It	**can**	**drive**	a car.
We			
You			
They			

NEGATIVE STATEMENTS			
SUBJECT	**CAN + NOT**	**BASE FORM OF VERB**	
I			
You			
He She It	**cannot can't**	**drive**	a car.
We			
You			
They			

YES/NO QUESTIONS		
CAN	**SUBJECT**	**BASE FORM OF VERB**
Can	you	**dance**?
	she	
	they	

SHORT ANSWERS					
YES	**SUBJECT**	**CAN**	**NO**	**SUBJECT**	**CAN'T**
Yes,	I	**can**.	No,	I	**can't**.
	she			she	
	they			they	

INFORMATION QUESTIONS				ANSWERS
WH- WORD	**CAN**	**SUBJECT**	**BASE FORM OF VERB**	
Who	can	you	**trust?**	I **can** only trust Paulo.
What			**play?**	The piano and the violin.

▶ *Could* for Past Ability

AFFIRMATIVE STATEMENTS			NEGATIVE STATEMENTS		
SUBJECT	**COULD**	**BASE FORM OF VERB**	**SUBJECT**	**COULD + NOT**	**BASE FORM OF VERB**
I			I		
You			You		
He She It	could	swim.	He She It	could not couldn't	swim.
We			We		
You			You		
They			They		

YES/NO QUESTIONS			SHORT ANSWERS						
COULD	**SUBJECT**	**BASE FORM OF VERB**	**YES**	**SUBJECT**	**COULD**		**NO**	**SUBJECT**	**COULDN'T**
Could	you	swim?	Yes,	I	could.		No,	I	couldn't.
	she			she				she	
	they			they				they	

INFORMATION QUESTIONS				ANSWERS
WH- WORD	**COULD**	**SUBJECT**	**BASE FORM OF VERB**	
When	could	he	**walk?**	At 11 months.
What			**do?**	He **could** read and write.

Can and *Could*
- *Can* and *could* are modal verbs.
- Like all modals, *can* and *could* come before the base form of the verb. They also have the same form with all subjects.

(Continued on page 310)

- *Cannot* is the negative form of *can*. *Can't* is the contraction.
- *Could not* is the negative of *could*. *Couldn't* is the contraction.
- In affirmative sentences with *can* and *could*, we stress the main verb. We do not stress *can* or *could*. The vowel sound in both words is very short.

    I can gȯ. — I /kən/ go.   I could gȯ. — I /kəd/ go.

- In negative sentences with *can* and *could*, we stress *can't* and *couldn't*. We pronounce the *a* in *can't* like the *a* in *ant*. We pronounce the *ou* in *couldn't* like the *oo* in *good*.

    I can't gȯ. — I /kænt/ go.   I couldn't gȯ. — I /ˈkʊdnt/ go.

B1 Listening for Form

CD2 T25 **Listen to the conversation. Write the form of *can* or *could* you hear.**

Dan: My brother is really smart. He's only six and he ____can____ read the newspaper.
  ₁

Amy: Well, my cousin Susan is smart, too. She's sixteen years old, and she just graduated from college. She _____ speak five languages. She _____
  ₂ ₃
read at the age of three, and she _____ do high school math in elementary
  ₄
school.

Dan: Wow! Some people _____ do elementary school math in high school!
  ₅

Amy: Life isn't always easy for Susan. She _____ talk to professors, but she
  ₆
_____ talk to other teenagers. She doesn't know what to say to them. She
  ₇
_____ be in class with kids her own age, so she never had many friends.
  ₈

Dan: Was she lonely?

Amy: Yes. She _____ read and talk to adults, but she _____ be just a kid.
  ₉ ₁₀

B2 Forming Sentences with *Can* and *Can't*

Form sentences with *can* and *can't*, and write them in your notebook. Use the words and phrases. Punctuate your sentences correctly.

1. David/drive/can/his father's/car

    David can drive his father's car.

2. can't/Teresa/speak/Spanish

3. cannot/swim/Irina/very well

4. Julie/the piano/play/and/the guitar/can

5. eat/can't/solid food/the baby

6. Tomek/fast/run/can't/very

310 | **CHAPTER 20** *Can and Could* for Present and Past Ability

B3 Forming Questions with *Can*

Form *Yes/No* questions and information questions with *can*, and write them in your notebook. Use the words and phrases. Punctuate your sentences correctly.

1. you/swim/can

    Can you swim?

2. languages/you/speak/can/many

3. play/any instruments/can/Hanna

4. ride/a bicycle/can/you

5. what/cook/can/Alex

6. who/me/can/beat/at tennis

B4 Working on *Could* and *Couldn't*

A. Eva was a child prodigy. Look at the information in the chart. Write sentences in your notebook about what Eva could and could not do as a four-year-old child. Punctuate your sentences correctly.

    Eva could speak Mandarin.

	COMPARATIVE	YES	NO
1.	speak Mandarin	✓	
2.	roller-skate		✓
3.	tie her shoes		✓
4.	draw beautiful pictures	✓	
5.	ride a bicycle		✓
6.	play the piano	✓	
7.	play tennis		✓
8.	write simple poetry	✓	

B. With a partner look back at the information in the chart in part A. Take turns asking and answering *Yes/No* questions with *could*. Respond with short answers.

    A: *Could Eva speak Mandarin?*
    B: *Yes, she could.*

MEANING AND USE

Present and Past Ability

Think Critically About Meaning and Use

A. Read the sentences and answer the questions below.

   a. I can't remember her address.
   b. Hiro could speak Japanese and Korean at the age of eight.
   c. Can you name five twentieth-century American writers?
   d. Could you write your name at the age of four?

   1. EVALUATE Which sentences refer to present ability?

   2. EVALUATE Which sentences refer to past ability?

B. Discuss your answers with the class and read the Meaning and Use Notes to check them.

Meaning and Use Notes

ONLINE PRACTICE

Present Ability with *Can*

▶ 1   Use *can* and *can't* to talk about ability in the present. An ability is something you know how to do.

   I **can run** four miles in an hour.   She **can do** math problems in her head.

   She **can't climb** trees! She's 85!   We **can't speak** French very well.

Past Ability with *Could*

▶ 2   Use *could* and *couldn't* to talk about ability in the past.

   I **could ride** a bike at age 5.   My uncle **could** still **roller-skate** at 75!

   They **couldn't read** in kindergarten.   He got lost because he **couldn't speak** French.

C1 Listening for Meaning and Use

▶ Notes 1, 2

CD2 T26   Listen to each situation. Choose the statement that is true.

1. **a.** John can ski well.

   b. John can't ski.

2. **a.** He can't hear the teacher.

   b. He can hear the teacher.

3. **a.** John Wayne can act well.

   b. John Wayne could act well.

4. **a.** They can't read Japanese.

   b. They couldn't read Japanese.

5. **a.** She can't make a cake.

   b. She couldn't make a cake.

6. **a.** He couldn't wake up on time.

   b. He can't wake up on time.

7. **a.** They can both play instruments.

   b. They could both play instruments.

8. **a.** He can't see the board.

   b. He couldn't see the board.

C2 Talking About Present Abilities

▶ Note 1

A. Work in groups of four. Write the names of your three partners at the top of the chart. Then take turns asking and answering questions about the activities in the chart. Check (✓) the things you and your classmates can do. Record the results in the Totals column.

A: Can you ride a bike?   *B: Yes, I can.*

	BASE FORM	ME	_____	_____	_____	TOTAL
1.	ride a bike	✓				
2.	drive a car					
3.	swim					
4.	play the piano					
5.	speak three languages					
6.	do 100 sit-ups					
7.	bake cookies					
8.	type 50 words a minute					
9.	ski					
10.	fly an airplane					

B. Compare your totals with the other groups. What can a lot of people do? What can only a few people do?

C3 Talking About Past Ability

▶ Note 2

A. Complete the sentences. Use *could* or *couldn't* to make true statements.

1. At five years old I ___I couldn't swim___.

2. At the age of ten _____.

3. Ten years ago _____.

4. In my first English class _____.

5. On my first day at school _____.

6. At the end of first grade _____.

B. Discuss your answers with a partner.

A: At five years old I couldn't swim.
B: I could!

C4 Contrasting Past and Present Ability

▶ Notes 1, 2

Complete the paragraph. Use *can, can't, could,* or *couldn't*.

Five years ago some of my friends ___could___ drive, but I _____ . This was a problem
because I lived on a farm in those days, and I _____ go many places on my own. Last year I got my driver's license. Today I _____ drive, but I still _____ go places by car because I don't own one. I'm not complaining, though. I live in a big city now, and I _____ go everywhere by bus or subway. Back on the farm, I _____ take buses or trains because there was no public transportation in my area. I visited a few neighbors on my bike, but I _____ cycle to town. It was just too far away.

Think Critically About Meaning and Use

A. Complete each conversation.

1. A: Could you swim at the age of six?

B: _____

a. No, I couldn't.

b. No, I can't.

c. Yes, I can.

2. A: _____

B: No, not anymore.

a. When can you play the piano?

b. Can you play the piano?

c. Who can play for us?

3. A: Can you speak Russian?

B: _____

a. No, I studied German.

b. No, I'm not.

c. Yes, I am.

4. A: Why were you afraid of the water?

B: _____

a. I can swim.

b. I couldn't swim.

c. I am swimming.

B. Discuss these questions in small groups.

1. **EVALUATE** Why is *could* used in 1 in both question and the answer?

2. **DRAW A CONCLUSION** In 2, what is true about speaker B? (Circle the letter of the correct answer.)

a. He couldn't play the piano in the past.

b. He could play the piano in the past.

Edit

Some of these sentences have errors. Find the errors and correct them.

1. We ~~can't~~ *can't* leave right now.

2. They can to see in the dark.

3. She can runs very quickly.

4. She was very fit. She could do 100 sit-ups.

5. Could he spoke German?

6. What you can cook?

7. She cans sing and dance.

8. Greg is bilingual. He can't speak two languages.

Write

Write a paragraph about your abilities in the past and your abilities today. Use *can* and *could*.

1. **BRAINSTORM** List all the things you could do when you were a child and all the things you can do now. Use these questions to make notes.
   - What things could you do as a five-year-old child?
   - Did you have any special athletic or academic abilities?
   - What things couldn't you do?
   - What things can you do now?
   - What things can't you do now?
   - Do you have any special athletic or academic abilities?
   - Do you have any job-related abilities?

2. **WRITE A FIRST DRAFT** Before you write your first draft, read the checklist below. Write your draft using modals.

3. **EDIT** Read your work and check it against the checklist below. Circle grammar, spelling, and punctuation errors.

DO I ...	YES
use *can* to show present ability?	☐
use *could* to show past ability?	☐
make affirmative and negative statements using *can* and *could*?	☐
ask and answer *Yes/No* questions using *can* and *could*?	☐
ask and answer information questions using *can* and *could*?	☐

4. **PEER REVIEW** Work with a partner to help you decide how to fix your errors and improve the content.

5. **REWRITE YOUR DRAFT** Using the comments from your partner, write a final draft.

> As a five-year-old child, I didn't have many special abilities.
> I could say the alphabet and I could write my name, but I
> couldn't read or write properly. Now, however, I can write my
> name, of course, and I can also write long reports and letters...

21

Modals of Request and Permission

Standing Up for Yourself

A1 Before You Read

Discuss these questions.

Do you always express your true feelings, or do you hide your feelings?

A2 Read

 CD2 T27 Read this newspaper interview. Dr. Grey talks about three types of people. What are they? Which type of person are you?

Books

Standing Up for Yourself

Our reviewer, Paul Harris, spoke with Dr. Stanley Grey, the author of *Standing Up for Yourself.* Here is part of the conversation.

5   **HARRIS:** Dr. Grey, your new book is about assertiveness. <u>Can you explain the term?</u>

GREY: Of course. Assertiveness means expressing your feelings and needs 10 honestly. Americans generally value assertiveness. However, sometimes people confuse assertiveness with aggression.

HARRIS: <u>Could you tell us the</u> 15 <u>difference between aggressive and assertive people?</u>

GREY: Sure. Aggressive people are often rude. They think about their own needs, and they don't care about the 20 needs of others. This makes others feel hurt or angry. Assertive people respect the needs of other people, but they also express their own needs so others can respect them in return.

25   **HARRIS:** <u>Would you give us an example?</u>

GREY: Of course. Say it's your birthday and your family is having a special dinner for you at 6:00. At 4:30 your 30 boss says: "I need your help. <u>Will you work until 8:00?</u>" An unassertive person will call home and apologize, then stay and do the work. An aggressive person might say, "No, I won't. my hours are 35 9:00 to 5:00. I have plans after work." This is rude and will also make the boss angry. An assertive person might say,

"Could I come in early tomorrow and do the work then?"

40 **HARRIS:** How can we become more assertive?

GREY: Well, you can start with these three tips:

1. Be open about your needs. Suppose
45 your term paper is due tomorrow
    and your computer doesn't work. Ask
    a friend for help. Say, "My paper is
    due tomorrow and my computer is
    broken. Can I use yours?" Your

50 friend may need the computer, too.
    Ask another person if necessary.

2. Be honest about your feelings. Your
   roommate loves jazz, but you don't.
   Don't pretend you do. Say, "Can you
55 use your earphones, please? I don't
   want to listen to jazz right now."

3. Say no to unreasonable requests.
   Your best friend asks, "May I wear
   your new sweater tonight?" Don't say
60 yes just to be polite. Say, "I'm sorry, I
   want to wear it first. Do you want to
   borrow another one?"

---

aggressive: ready to argue or fight or to use force

assertive: expressing your feelings and needs clearly and firmly

respect: to think highly of, care about

rude: not polite

standing up for yourself: protecting your feelings or needs

unassertive: not expressing your feelings and needs

value: to think something is good, to appreciate

A3 After You Read

Read each situation. Write *UN* for unassertive, *AG* for aggressive, or *AS* for assertive.

_UN_ **1.** John's roommate borrowed his new CD player and broke it. John is upset. He says, "Don't worry. I can buy another one."

_____ **2.** Jenny's friend wants to go to a horror movie. Jenny hates horror movies. She says, "Horror movies give me bad dreams. Can we see something else?"

_____ **3.** Tamika's brother wants her to help him with his homework. She says, "Do it yourself!"

_____ **4.** Jorge is very busy. His mother asks him to go to the store. He says, "I'd like to finish this first. Can I go later?"

_____ **5.** Fumiko's best friend asks to borrow some money. Fumiko is worried about money herself. She says, "Sure. No problem."

_____ **6.** A classmate asks to copy Rob's homework. Rob spent three hours doing it. He says, "I'm sorry, but I don't share my work."

B FORM

Modals of Request and Permission

Think Critically About Form

A. Look back at the interview on pages 318–319 and complete the tasks below.

1. **ANALYZE** Look at the underlined questions. Find the modal of request in each question. What subject do the questions have in common? Does the modal come before or after the subject?

2. **ANALYZE** Look at the circled questions. Find the modal of permission in each question. What subject do the questions have in common? Does the modal come before or after the subject?

B. Discuss your answers with the class and read the Form charts to check them.

▶ Modals Of Request: *Can, Could, Will, Would*

ONLINE
PRACTICE

	YES/NO QUESTIONS				SHORT ANSWERS					
MODAL	SUBJECT	BASE FORM OF VERB		YES	SUBJECT	CAN/ WILL	NO	SUBJECT	CAN/WILL + NOT
Can	you	explain	that?	Yes,	I	can.	No,	I	can't.
Could									
Will						will.			won't.
Would									

- We generally use modals of request in questions with *you*.
- We usually use *can* and *will* in affirmative short answers. *Could* and *would* are less common.
- The short answer *I won't* can sound angry and impolite. Do not use it in polite answers.
- We often use *please* in *Yes/No* questions with modals of request. *Please* can come at the end of a sentence or after the subject. In written English, we use a comma before *please* if it comes at the end of a sentence.

  Could you explain that, **please**?   Would <u>you</u> **please** explain that?

▶ Modals Of Permission: *Can, Could, May*

AFFIRMATIVE STATEMENTS			
SUBJECT	*CAN/MAY*	BASE FORM OF VERB	
You	**can**	sit	here.
	may		

NEGATIVE STATEMENTS			
SUBJECT	*CAN/MAY* + *NOT*	BASE FORM OF VERB	
You	**cannot** **can't**	sit	here.
	may not		

YES/NO QUESTIONS			
MODAL	SUBJECT	BASE FORM OF VERB	
Can	I we	**borrow**	your car?
Could			
May			

SHORT ANSWERS						
YES	SUBJECT	*CAN/ MAY*		*NO*	SUBJECT	*CAN/MAY + NOT*
Yes,	you	**can**.		No,	you	**cannot**. **can't**.
		may.				**may not**.

INFORMATION QUESTIONS				
WH- WORD	MODAL	SUBJECT	BASE FORM OF VERB	
What	**can**	I we	**call**	you?
Where	**may**		**park**	the car?
When	**could**		**visit**	you?

ANSWERS
You **can call** me Rob.
You **may park** in the driveway.
Next month.

- We generally use modals of permission in questions with *I* or *we*.
- Use *can* and *may* in statements. Do not use *could*.
- Use *can*, *could*, and *may* in *Yes/No* questions. Do not use *could* in short answers.
- There is no contracted form of *may not*.
- We often use *please* in *Yes/No* questions with modals of permission. *Please* can come at the end of a sentence or after the subject. In written English, we use a comma before *please* if it comes at the end of a sentence.

    Could I borrow your car, **please**?   May we **please** borrow your car?

B1 Listening for Form

CD2 T28 Listen to each sentence. What modal do you hear? Check (✓) the correct column.

	CAN	COULD	MAY	WILL	WOULD
1.					✓
2.					
3.					
4.					
5.					
6.					
7.					
8.					

B2 Forming Statements and Questions

A. Form statements with modals of permission and write them in your notebook. Use the words. Punctuate your sentences correctly.

1. take/you/not/the/may/tomorrow/test

    You may not take the test tomorrow.

2. park/you/here/can't/car/your

3. early/you/leave/may/not

4. may/my/computer/borrow/they

5. can't/you/talk/him/to/now

B. Form questions with modals of request and permission and write them in your notebook. Use the words. Punctuate your sentences correctly.

1. you/me/could/please/help

    Could you help me, please? OR *Could you please help me?*

2. ride/us/can/give/a/you

3. close/the/you/would/please/door

4. have/could/time/I/more/please

5. can/when/call/I/him

B3 Working on Short Answers

Complete each conversation with a subject pronoun and *can, will,* or *can't.*

1. **A:** Can I take the test tomorrow?

   B: No, _____you can't_____ . Today is the last day of the semester.

2. **A:** Will you teach me to play chess?

   B: Yes, _____ . Where's the board?

3. **A:** Could you tell me the time?

   B: No, _____ . I don't have my watch.

4. **A:** Can I borrow a pen?

   B: Yes, _____ .

5. **A:** Can we play outside, Mom?

   B: Yes, _____ , but don't cross the street.

6. **A:** Could I see the newspaper, please?

   B: Yes, _____ .

7. **A:** Would you take care of my cat while I'm gone?

   B: Yes, _____ . No problem.

8. **A:** Could you bring me a piece of apple pie, please?

   B: No, _____ . There isn't any more. Could I get you something else instead?

   A: Yes, _____ . Do you have any chocolate cake?

9. **A:** Professor Brown, could you please write a letter of recommendation for me?

   B: Yes, _____ . It will be a pleasure.

10. **A:** Will you take out the trash?

    B: No, _____ . I'm waiting for an important phone call.

MEANING AND USE

Making Requests and Asking for Permission

 Think Critically About Meaning and Use

A. Read the sentences and answer the questions below.

a. Can I borrow this book?
b. Would you carry these books for me?
c. May I use this glass?

d. Could I borrow your jacket tonight?
e. Will you tell the teacher I'm sick?
f. Could you lend me ten dollars?

1. **CATEGORIZE** Which sentences make a request for someone to do something?

2. **CATEGORIZE** Which sentences ask someone for permission?

B. Discuss your answers with the class and read the Meaning and Use Notes to check them.

Meaning and Use Notes

ONLINE PRACTICE

Making Requests

▶1 Use *can, could, will,* and *would* to ask someone to do something. We usually use *can* and *will* in less formal conversations, with friends and family. *Could* and *would* make a request sound more polite. We use them in more formal conversations, with strangers or people in authority.

Less Formal

To a Friend: **Can** you hold this for me?

To a Child: **Will** you clean your room?

More Formal

To a Stranger: **Could** you tell me the time?

To Your Boss: **Would** you sign this?

Agreeing to and Refusing Requests

▶2 We generally use *can* and *will* to agree to a request. *Could* and *would* are less common. We often use *can't* and *won't* to refuse a request. *Won't* is very strong and sounds impolite.

Agreeing to a Request

A: Could you take Amy to school?

B: Yes, I **can**.

A: Would you go to the post office?

B: Yes, I **will**.

Refusing a Request

A: Dan, **will** you answer the door?

B: Sorry, I **can't**. I'm on the phone. (polite)

A: Ava, will you answer the phone?

B: No, I **won't**! You answer it! (impolite)

Asking for Permission

▶ **3** Use *can*, *could*, and *may* to ask for permission. *Can* and *could* are less formal than *may*. *May* sounds more formal and polite. We often use *may* when we speak to strangers or people in authority.

Less Formal

Son to Father: **Can/Could** I go out tonight?

More Formal

Stranger to Stranger: **May** I sit here?

Giving and Refusing Permission

▶ **4** Use *can* or *may* to give permission. Do not use *could*. Use *may not*, *can't*, and *cannot* to refuse permission. *May* and *may not* are more formal.

Giving Permission

A: Can I use your computer?

B: Yes, you **can**. (less formal)

A: May I take the test tomorrow?

B: Yes, you **may**. (more formal)

Refusing Permission

A: Can I give you the report tomorrow?

B: No, you **can't**. Sorry. (less formal)

A: May I borrow the car?

B: No, you **may not**. I need it. (more formal)

Using *Please*, *Sorry*, and Other Expressions

▶ **5A** Use *please* to make questions sound more polite.

Making a Request

Will you **please** open the door for me?

Could you answer the phone, **please**?

Asking for Permission

May I **please** have a glass of water?

Could I talk to you, **please**?

▶ **5B** Use *I'm sorry* or *sorry* and an excuse to make refusals sound softer and more polite.

Refusing a Request

A: Could you drive me to the mall later?

B: **Sorry**, I have a doctor's appointment.

Refusing Permission

A: Can I borrow your bike?

B: I'm **sorry**, I lent it to Dan.

▶ **5C** We often use expressions such as *sure*, *OK*, *certainly*, or *of course* to agree to requests and give permission.

Agreeing to a Request

A: Would you take Amy to school?

B: **Sure** I will.

A: Could you go to the store for me?

B: **OK**.

Giving Permission

A: Can I borrow your pen?

B: **Certainly**.

A: May I sit here?

B: **Of course**. Go right ahead.

C1 Listening for Meaning and Use

▶ Notes 1, 3

CD2 T29 Listen to each question. Is the speaker making a request or asking for permission? Check (✓) the correct column.

	PERMISSION	REQUEST
1.	✓	
2.		
3.		
4.		
5.		
6.		

C2 Making and Responding to Requests

▶ Notes 1, 2, 5A–5C

Complete the conversations. Use appropriate modals and appropriate responses. Make at least two refusals.

Conversation 1: Paulo is in a clothing store.

Paulo: _Could_ you help me, please?

Clerk: _Of course I can. What size do you wear?_ _____

Conversation 2: Josh and his friends are in a restaurant.

Josh: _____ you give us a table near the window?

Waiter: _____

Conversation 3: Sally and Ruth are taking a test.

Ruth: Sally, _____ you tell me the answer to number 2?

Sally: _____

Conversation 4: Irina is on a public bus.

Irina: Driver, _____ you stop at the next corner, please?

Driver: _____

Conversation 5: Corey is at home.

Corey: Mom, _____ you make lasagna for dinner tonight?

Mom: _____

C3 Asking for Permission

▶ Notes 3, 4, 5A–5C

A. Write a question with *can*, *could*, or *may* to ask permission in each situation. Use explanations and polite expressions when appropriate. Use each modal at least once. Punctuate your sentences correctly.

1. You are at work. You have a doctor's appointment. Ask your boss for permission to take a long lunch break.

   I have a doctor's appointment. Could I take a long lunch break today?

   _____

2. You are in line at the bank. You don't have a pen. The man in front of you is writing a check. Ask to borrow his pen.

   _____

   _____

3. You are in a restaurant. You need another chair at your table. Ask the person at the next table for permission to take an empty chair.

   _____

   _____

4. You are at home. You have an important message for your friend Rosa Gomez. You call her home and her father answers. Ask to talk to Rosa.

   _____

   _____

5. Your computer isn't working. You have to write a paper. Ask to use your roommate's computer.

   _____

   _____

6. You need to go grocery shopping. Ask your friend Marcus for permission to use his car.

   _____

   _____

B. Work with a partner. Take turns asking and answering your questions in part A.

   A: Could I have a long lunch break today? I have a doctor's appointment.

   B: Certainly, go right ahead. OR *I'm sorry, you can't. Did you forget about the big meeting?*

C4 Making Requests and Asking for Permission

▶ Notes 1–5C

Write a short dialogue for each situation. For A, make a request or ask for permission. For B, write a response. More than one answer is possible.

1. A: _Can I borrow the car?_

    B: _No, you can't._

4. A: _____

    B: _____

2. A: _____

    B: _____

5. A: _____

    B: _____

3. A: _____

    B: _____

6. A: _____

    B: _____

WRITING   Write About Asking for Permission

Think Critically About Meaning and Use

A. Complete each conversation.

1. A: _____

B: Sorry, I can't. This is my only one.

    (a.) Can you lend me a pen, please?

    b. Can you get a pen?

    c. Will you buy a pen?

2. A: How can I help you?

B: _____

    a. Yes, you can.

    b. I'm looking for a white blouse.

    c. I'm a customer.

3. A: May I please use the phone?

B: _____

    a. Of course you may.

    b. Sorry, you won't.

    c. Sure you will.

4. A: _____

B: No, you had pizza last night.

    a. Could you have pizza for dinner?

    b. Can we have pizza for dinner?

    c. When may we have pizza?

B. Discuss these questions in small groups.

1. ANALYZE In 3, what two words make speaker A's question a polite request?

2. EVALUATE In 4, why do you think speaker A doesn't use these polite words?

Edit

Some of these sentences have errors. Find the errors and correct them.

Could

1. ~~Will~~ I borrow your car?

2. No, you mayn't smoke here.

3. Where can we sit?

4. Would I leave now, please?

5. May you help me?

6. Would please you help me?

7. Will you open the door, please?

8. Sure, I can't help you now. I'm busy.

Write

Write a conversation about an employee who is asking his boss for permission to do something. Use modals of request and permission.

1. **BRAINSTORM** Think of a situation where an employee wants to do something but the boss doesn't want to let the employee do it. Use these questions to make notes.

   - What is the situation?
   - What does the employee want?
   - How will the employee ask for this?
   - Why does the boss want the employee to stay at work?
   - What would the employee say in response to the boss?
   - How will the boss respond to the request?
   - How would the boss respond positively?
   - How would the boss respond negatively?

2. **WRITE A FIRST DRAFT** Before you write your first draft, read the checklist below. Write your draft using modals.

3. **EDIT** Read your work and check it against the checklist below. Circle grammar, spelling, and punctuation errors.

DO I ...	YES
use modals of request and permission?	☐
make affirmative and negative statements?	☐
ask and answer *yes/no* questions using modals of request and permission?	☐
ask and answer information questions using modals of request and permission?	☐
include long and short answers?	☐
include questions asking for permission?	☐
use *please* and other expressions to be polite?	☐

4. **PEER REVIEW** Work with a partner to help you decide how to fix your errors and improve the content.

5. **REWRITE YOUR DRAFT** Using the comments from your partner, write a final draft.

> A: Mike, I want to go to night school. May I adjust my schedule so that I can leave early to attend classes?
>
> B: I don't like the idea of you leaving work early, but I think it's a good idea to further your education. So it's okay to attend, but you should get your work done before you leave the office.
>
> A: No problem, I can do that!

22

Modals of Advice, Necessity, and Prohibition

Rule Followers and Rule Breakers

A1 Before You Read

 Discuss these questions.

What do you think about rules? Are they necessary? Do you usually follow rules? Why or why not?

A2 Read

CD2 T30 Read and complete this quiz from a magazine. Are you a rule follower or a rule breaker?

Rule Followers
and **Rule Breakers**

There are two kinds of people in the world: people who follow rules and people who break them. Rule followers think that every rule exists for a good reason, even if they don't
5 know what it is. They think that people should always follow the rules. One of my friends is a rule follower. He says, "Rules are important. We have to follow them. Rules make life orderly." Another friend of mine hates rules.
10 His philosophy? He thinks that he doesn't have to follow rules that are unreasonable. He says, "A person should only obey rules that make sense."

What do you think? Are you a rule follower, a rule breaker, or somewhere
15 **in between? Take the following quiz and find out.**

1 You're standing at a corner and waiting to cross the street. There aren't any cars on the road, but the sign says, "Don't Walk." What
20 should you do?

   a. You should wait.

   b. You should cross the street.

   c. You should look both ways, then cross the street.

25 **2** What does a stop sign mean to you?

   a. Every car must stop.

   b. The car behind your car has to stop.

30   **c.** You have to slow down and be careful.

3 You're at a swimming pool and you see a sign that says, "No Running." What does this mean
35 to you?

   a. You must not run.

   b. Other people shouldn't run.

   c. You have to run carefully.

4 On the first day of class your
40 teacher says, "Students must spend at least an hour a week in the language lab." You …

   a. sign up for an hour of lab time each week.

45   **b.** don't think you need an hour, so you sign up for half an hour.

   c. check the lab schedule and decide to go when you have time.

5 You ride your bike to the store.
50 A sign says, "Do NOT park bikes here." You don't see any other place to park your bike and you don't want it to get stolen. What should you do?

55   **a.** You go home because there is no place to park your bike.

   b. You park your bike right in front of the sign that says, "Do NOT park bikes here."

60   **c.** You park your bike on the other side of the street.

KEY

➤ **Mostly *a* answers:** You're a rule follower.

➤ **Mostly *b* answers:** You're a rule breaker.

➤ **Mostly *c* answers:** You sometimes follow rules and sometimes break them.

---

philosophy: a set of beliefs
to make sense: to be logical

unreasonable: not logical

A3 After You Read

 Compare your answers to the quiz with four other students. Who is most like you?

B FORM

Should, Must, and *Have To*

Think Critically About Form

A. Look back at the quiz on pages 332–333 and complete the tasks below.

1. **IDENTIFY** Look at the underlined examples of *should* + verb and *must* + verb. What is the subject of each example? Do *should* and *must* have different forms with different subjects? What form of the verb follows *should* and *must*?

2. **IDENTIFY** Look at the circled examples of the phrasal modal *have to* + verb. What is the subject of each sentence? Does *have to* have different forms with different subjects? What form of the verb follows *have to*?

B. Discuss your answers with the class and read the Form charts to check them.

▶ *Should/Must*

ONLINE
PRACTICE

AFFIRMATIVE STATEMENTS		
SUBJECT	***SHOULD/MUST***	**BASE FORM OF VERB**
I		
You		
He She It	**should must**	**leave.**
We		
You		
They		

NEGATIVE STATEMENTS		
SUBJECT	***SHOULD/MUST + NOT***	**BASE FORM OF VERB**
I		
You		
He She It	**should not shouldn't must not**	**leave.**
We		
You		
They		

YES/NO QUESTIONS		
SHOULD	**SUBJECT**	**BASE FORM OF VERB**
Should	I she we	**leave?**

SHORT ANSWERS					
YES	**SUBJECT**	***SHOULD***	***NO***	**SUBJECT**	***SHOULD + NOT***
Yes,	you she we	**should.**	**No,**	you she we	**shouldn't.**

INFORMATION QUESTIONS				ANSWERS
WH- WORD	SHOULD	SUBJECT	BASE FORM OF VERB	
What	**should**	I	**do**?	Talk to your boss.
		she		She **should** work harder.

- *Should* and *must* are modals. Like all modals, they come before the base form of the verb. They also have the same form with all subjects.
- The form *mustn't* is not very common in American English.
- In questions, *have to* (see below) is more common than *must*.

▶ Have To

AFFIRMATIVE STATEMENTS		
SUBJECT	HAVE TO	BASE FORM OF VERB
I	**have to**	
You		
She	**has to**	**leave**.
We		
You	**have to**	
They		

NEGATIVE STATEMENTS			
SUBJECT	DO/DOES + NOT	HAVE TO	BASE FORM OF VERB
I	**don't**		
You			
She	**doesn't**	**have to**	**leave**.
We			
You	**don't**		
They			

YES/NO QUESTIONS			
DO/DOES	SUBJECT	HAVE TO	BASE FORM OF VERB
Do	I	**have to**	**leave**?
Does	she		

SHORT ANSWERS					
YES	SUBJECT	DO/DOES	NO	SUBJECT	DO/DOES + NOT
Yes,	you	**do**.	No,	you	**don't**.
	he	**does**.		he	**doesn't**.

INFORMATION QUESTIONS					ANSWERS
WH- WORD	DO/DOES	SUBJECT	HAVE TO	BASE FORM OF VERB	
When	**do**	we	**have to**	**study**?	Tomorrow.
What	**does**	she			Chapter 24.

(Continued on page 336)

- *Have to* is different from *should* and *must*. It is not a true modal. It has a different form for the third-person singular.

  You **have to** call him.   She **has** to call him.

- *Have to* has no contracted form.

- We use *do* with *have to* in negative statements and questions.

  I **don't have** to call him.   **Do** I **have to** call him?

- *Have to* usually replaces *must* in questions.

  Do I **have to** be home by 10:00 P.M.?

B1 Listening for Form

CD2 T31 Listen to each conversation. Which modal do you hear? Check (✓) the correct column.

	(DON'T) HAVE TO	MUST (NOT)	SHOULD (NOT)
1.	✓		
2.			
3.			
4.			
5.			
6.			

B2 Building Sentences with *Should, Must,* and *Have To*

Build four affirmative and four negative sentences. Use a word or phrase from each column. You may omit the second and fourth column in some of your sentences. Punctuate your sentences correctly.

I must take the test.

I		must		take the test
you	(don't)	should		make a speech
the other students	(doesn't)	have to	(not)	go by plane
Susan		has to		study tonight

B3 Forming *Yes/No* Questions with *Should* and *Have To*

Form *Yes/No* questions with *should* and *have to*. Use the words and phrases. Remember to add *do* or *does* if necessary. Punctuate your sentences correctly.

1. we/watch a movie tonight/should

   <u>Should we watch a movie tonight?</u>

2. you/go to class tomorrow/have to

   _____

3. your friend/study chemistry next year/have to

   _____

4. we/have homework on the weekends/should

   _____

5. the school library/be open all night/should

   _____

B4 Writing Information Questions with *Should* and *Have To*

Write information questions with *should* and *have to*. Use the responses and question words to help you. Punctuate your questions correctly.

1. **A:** <u>What time should young children go to bed?</u> (what time)

   B: Young children should go to bed at eight o'clock.

2. **A:** _____ (what)

   B: We have to read Chapter 6 for tomorrow.

3. **A:** _____ (who)

   B: The accountants should check the deposits.

4. **A:** _____ (how long)

   B: You have to wait about two weeks for the test results.

5. **A:** _____ (when)

   B: Mr. and Mrs. Jones have to leave at noon.

C MEANING AND USE

Modals of Advice, Necessity, and Prohibition

Think Critically About Meaning and Use

A. Read the sentences and answer the questions below.

a. You should watch movies in English. You will improve your listening skills.
b. Wait a minute. I have to answer the phone.
c. You must not park here. It's a no parking zone.
d. You must take two writing courses in order to graduate.

1. ANALYZE Which sentence gives advice?

2. ANALYZE Which sentence says that something is not allowed?

3. COMPARE AND CONTRAST Which two sentences say that something is necessary? Which one is more formal?

B. Discuss your answers with the class and read the Meaning and Use Notes to check them.

Meaning and Use Notes

ONLINE PRACTICE

	Giving Advice and Expressing Opinions
▶ **1A**	Use *should* to give advice.
	You **should study** for the test tonight. He **shouldn't go** to the park this weekend.
▶ **1B**	Use *should* to express opinions.
	Everyone **should exercise** regularly. People **shouldn't smoke** cigarettes.

	Expressing Necessity
▶ **2A**	Use *have to* and *must* to talk about something that is necessary. Use *must* in formal or more serious situations.
	We **have to leave** now. Class starts in five minutes!
	You **must ask** permission to leave work early.
▶ **2B**	Use *must* to express rules, laws, and requirements, especially in writing.
	Students **must pay** their tuition before the first day of class.

▶ **2C**   We often use *have to* instead of *must* to talk about rules and laws in conversation.

We **have to pay** our tuition today. The business office is open until 8:00 P.M.

You **have to wear** your seatbelt at all times.

Expressing Lack of Necessity and Prohibition

▶ **3**   The negative forms of *must* and *have to* have very different meanings. *Don't/ doesn't have to* means that something is not necessary for you to do (but you can). *Must not* means that something is prohibited (you cannot do it). There is no choice.

Not Necessary

I'm on vacation. I **don't have to get up** early.

Prohibited

Visitors **must not** block the entrance.

C1 Listening for Meaning and Use

▶ Notes 1A–3

 CD2 T32   Listen to each statement. Choose the correct use of the modal.

1. necessity (opinion)

2. advice necessity

3. advice opinion

4. necessity lack of necessity

5. advice necessity

6. necessity prohibition

7. necessity lack of necessity

8. prohibition lack of necessity

C2 Giving Advice

▶ Notes 1,A–1B

Work with a partner. Read each situation. Take turns giving advice with *should* and *should not*.

1. Paulo is the coach of his soccer team. The team lost many games. Many members of the team feel discouraged. Some want to quit. What should Paulo do?

   He should have extra practice sessions. He shouldn't…

2. Linda wants to feel and look better. She works too hard. What should Linda do?

3. Brad is upset because his roommate plays loud music. It's difficult for Brad to study. Brad talked to his roommate, but it didn't make a difference. What should Brad do?

C3 Describing Rules and Requirements

A. Work with a partner. Study the chart and think about your school's rules and requirements. Check (✓) the correct column.

		REQUIRED	NOT REQUIRED	PROHIBITED
1.	be late for class			✓
2.	wear a uniform			
3.	buy a dictionary			
4.	eat in the classroom			
5.	talk in the computer lab			
6.	do homework			
7.	carry a student ID			
8.	pay school fees			

B. Write full sentences in your notebook to describe the rules and requirements at your school. Use the information in the chart. Use *must* and *must not* to describe rules and requirements. Use *don't have to* to describe what is not a rule or requirement.

Students must not be late for class.

Think Critically About Meaning and Use

A. Complete each conversation.

1. A: This is a dangerous neighborhood. _____

B: Don't worry. I'll be fine.

   (a.) You have to lock your door at night.

   b. You don't have to leave the windows open.

   c. You must not lock your apartment.

2. A: I'm hungry. I'm going to make a sandwich.

B: _____ We're meeting the Haddads at the restaurant in an hour.

   a. You have to eat.

   b. You must eat now.

   c. You shouldn't eat now.

3. A: We can't park here. Look at that sign.

B: You're right! _____

   a. Visitors must not use this lot.

   b. Visitors must park here.

   c. Visitors don't have to park here.

4. A: _____

B: Maybe a book. She loves to read.

   a. Do I have to get Susan a present for her birthday?

   b. What should I buy Susan for her graduation?

   c. Who should get Susan a birthday present?

B. Discuss these questions in small groups.

1. **EVALUATE** In 3, in what situation might we use each of the answer choices?

2. **INTERPRET** In 3, which choice expresses necessity? prohibition? lack of necessity?

Edit

Some of these sentences have errors. Find the errors and correct them.

1. We have _to_ leave tonight.

2. They must wear uniforms to school.

3. I should take chemistry next year.

4. U.S. voters should be at least 18 years old.

5. You must to finish before 6:00.

6. Does she has to leave immediately?

7. You should not studying every night.

8. Didn't you see the sign? You don't have to smoke here.

Write

Write a paragraph about the laws in your country. Use modals of advice, necessity, and prohibition.

1. **BRAINSTORM** List all the laws in your country that you can think of. Use these questions to help you.
   - Do people have to carry an ID with them?
   - Do drivers need to keep their driver's license in their car?
   - Do drivers have to have car insurance?
   - Do young men and women have to join the army?
   - Do adults have to vote in elections?
   - Do children have to attend school?
   - Do people have to pay taxes?

2. **WRITE A FIRST DRAFT** Before you write your first draft, read the checklist below. Write your draft using modals.

3. **EDIT** Read your work and check it against the checklist below. Circle grammar, spelling, and punctuation errors.

DO I ...	YES
use modals of advice, necessity, and prohibition?	☐
make affirmative and negative statements?	☐
ask and answer *Yes/No* questions using these modals?	☐
ask and answer information questions using these modals?	☐
include expressions of necessity?	☐
include expressions of prohibition?	☐
include descriptions of rules and requirements?	☐

4. **PEER REVIEW** Work with a partner to help you decide how to fix your errors and improve the content.

5. **REWRITE YOUR DRAFT** Using the comments from your partner, write a final draft.

> *All men and women over the age of 18 must carry an ID with them at all times. People must also have their driver's license with them when they drive...*

Choose the correct word or words to complete each sentence.

1. _____ I use your car tomorrow?

   a. Would   **b.** Can   **c.** Will   **d.** Won't

2. I'm sorry. You _____ borrow my book. I'm going to need it.

   a. wouldn't   **b.** won't   **c.** can't   **d.** couldn't

3. _____ I take this chair?

   a. Would   **b.** Must   **c.** Will   **d.** May

4. The concert is free. You _____ get a ticket.

   a. must not   **b.** don't have to   **c.** shouldn't   **d.** must

5. The train _____ be late. It sometimes is.

   a. might   **b.** is going   **c.** will   **d.** would

6. Can you _____ chess?

   a. played   **b.** playing   **c.** to play   **d.** play

7. The problem was very difficult. We _____ solve it.

   a. couldn't   **b.** can't   **c.** can   **d.** could

8. We _____ walk to Greg's house. It's only two blocks away.

   a. can't   **b.** must not   **c.** couldn't   **d.** can

Choose the correct response to complete each conversation.

9. **A:** What should I make for dinner?

  B: _____

     a. You don't have to.   **c.** Yes, you should.

     b. How about pasta?   **d.** No, not for dinner.

10. **A:** _____

   B: No, I don't. I'm going to go shopping.

     a. You shouldn't work this weekend.   **c.** Do you have to work this weekend?

     b. What should we do this weekend?   **d.** Do you have to go shopping this weekend?

11. **A:** What happened to John?

    B: _____

        a. He may be sick.

        b. He will be sick.

        c. He's going to be sick.

        d. He's always sick.

12. **A:** Can I open a window?

    B: _____

        a. No, you must open it.

        b. Sorry, you won't.

        c. Yes, you will.

        d. Sure, go right ahead.

13. **A:** Will you pass the salt, please?

    B: _____

        a. Of course.

        b. Sure you can.

        c. Yes, I may.

        d. Yes, you will.

14. **A:** Why did you get lost?

    B: _____

        a. I must read the map.

        b. The car can go very fast.

        c. We could get a taxi.

        d. I couldn't read the map.

Match the response to the statements below.

15. The baby is hungry.

16. The drive takes 17 hours.

17. My hands are freezing.

    a. You shouldn't do it in one day.

    b. We should water it.

    c. You should feed him.

    d. You shouldn't wait for me.

    e. You shouldn't stay up late.

    f. You should wear gloves.

Match the response to the questions below.

18. How is he going to the airport?

19. Can we go to the museum?

20. Why is the baby crying?

    a. He may take a taxi.

    b. He might not go.

    c. They might be lost.

    d. She might be hungry.

    e. I might not.

    f. She may.

    g. It may be closed today.

    h. It may rain later.

Object Pronouns; Direct and Indirect Objects

Holidays Around the World

A1 Before You Read

 Discuss these questions.

What is your favorite holiday? How do you celebrate this holiday?

A2 Read

CD2 T33 **Read this online article. How many holidays did you read about? Did you know about these holidays before you read the excerpt?**

Travel ▸ Articles

HOLIDAYS AROUND THE WORLD

All countries have special holidays. Some holidays are religious or cultural. Other holidays are political. Holidays around the world have many characteristics in common. On many holidays, people make special food for their friends and family. Often, they also give gifts to each other. For some holidays, people send cards to friends and
5 relatives, or sing special songs. Holidays are important because they teach children the traditions of their culture. Read below to learn what holidays some people around the world celebrate.

Day of the Dead (Mexico)

The Day of the Dead is not a sad holiday. On this day
10 (November 1), Mexicans remember their ancestors and tell their children stories about them. Everyone eats cookies and candy in the shape of skeletons, and decorates their houses with skeletons. Many Mexican families go to the cemetery on this day, too. Often they have a picnic at the
15 cemetery, and they offer food and drink to their ancestors. Families also clean the gravestones and plant flowers.

Shichi-Go-San (Japan)

Shichi-Go-San means "seven, five, three" in Japanese. This is a special celebration for children who are seven, five, and three years old. Families pray for the good health of
20 their children. Children are given *omiki*, a traditional drink. After that, the parents buy the children candy.

Boxing Day (Britain and Canada)

Boxing Day began hundreds of years ago in England. At that time, rich people gave boxes of gifts to their servants on December 26. Today, people in Britain and Canada
25 spend the day with family and friends. They eat a special meal of roast lamb or other meat.

Loy Krathong (Thailand)

On Loy Krathong, Thais make small boats from banana leaves. The boats usually contain a candle, flowers,
30 incense, and coins. In the evening, people carry their boats to the water. They light the candles and the incense. Then they make a wish and put their boats in the water. Thais believe that the boats will bring them happiness.

ancestors: relatives from a long time ago
cemetery: the place where people bury dead bodies
gravestones: stone markers on graves with the person's name, and dates of birth and death

incense: a substance that releases a pleasant smell when it burns
skeleton: the structure formed from all the bones of the body

A3 After You Read

Match the words and phrases to the correct holiday. Check (✓) the correct column.

		DAY OF THE DEAD	SHICHI-GO-SAN	BOXING DAY	LOY KRATHONG
1.	Mexico	✓			
2.	a holiday for children				
3.	remember ancestors				
4.	Thailand				
5.	Great Britain				
6.	give gifts to the servants				
7.	make boats				
8.	Japan				

B FORM 1

Object Pronouns

Think Critically About Form

A. Read the sentences and complete the tasks below.

1a. Call Mrs. Allen.   **2a.** I spoke to the manager.
1b. Call her.   **2b.** I spoke to him.

1. **IDENTIFY** An object follows a verb or a preposition. Underline the objects in the sentences.

2. **CATEGORIZE** Which objects are nouns? Which are pronouns?

B. Discuss your answers with the class and read the Form chart to check them.

ONLINE PRACTICE

OBJECT PRONOUNS		
SUBJECT PRONOUN	**OBJECT PRONOUN**	**EXAMPLES**
I	**me**	I helped my sister. She thanked **me**.
you	**you**	You will be late. I will drive **you**.
he	**him**	He needed some money. I helped **him**.
she	**her**	She is a ballerina. I admire **her**.
it	**it**	It is under the table. I can't find **it**.
we	**us**	We play soccer every day. Tom often joins **us**.
you	**you**	You need to work harder. I will help **you**.
they	**them**	They are outside. I'll get **them**.

- An object pronoun replaces a noun in the object position (after a verb in a sentence).
- When talking about a pair or group that includes you, mention yourself last.

  Brian talked to **him and me**.

Use *me* as the object of a verb or a preposition, not *I*.

My friend invited John and **me**.

X My friend invited John and I. (incorrect)

B1 Listening for Form

CD2 T34 Listen to the sentences. Check (✓) the object pronouns you hear.

	ME	HIM	HER	IT	US	THEM
1.						✓
2.						
3.						
4.						
5.						
6.						

B2 Working with Object Pronouns

Complete each sentence. Use the correct object pronoun related to the underlined noun.

1. <u>Diego</u> is worried. Please speak to _____him_____ .

2. There are <u>two new students</u> in class. We are waiting for _____ .

3. *Star Wars* is a good <u>movie</u>. I watched _____ last night.

4. <u>I</u> don't have a watch. Please tell _____ the time.

5. <u>Jack and I</u> are at home. Please call _____ .

6. <u>Elena</u> was sick yesterday. We visited _____ .

B3 Using Subject and Object Pronouns

Complete the paragraph. Use the correct subject pronouns and object pronouns.

In Muslim countries, _____we_____ have a three-day celebration called Eid el Fitr. The
                          1
celebration comes at the end of Ramadan, the month of fasting. On the first day of Eid

el Fitr, people make food and take _____ to their relatives' homes to eat together.
                                      2
Many parents buy their children new clothes for Eid el Fitr. The children wear

_____ on visits to their relatives and neighbors. When _____ was young, my
      3   4
mother always made a delicious dessert called *qatayef* for my brothers and me at

this time of year. My brothers and _____ liked to visit my grandmother during
                                        5
Eid el Fitr. _____ made _____ a big meal, and _____ always had a
                  6   7   8
great time.

Direct Objects and Indirect Objects

Think Critically About Form

A. Read the sentences and complete the tasks below.

  a. We sang a folk song.
  b. We sang it.
  c. We sang a folk song to the children.

  1. **IDENTIFY** Direct objects usually follow verbs. Underline the verb in each sentence. Circle the direct object.

  2. **RECOGNIZE** An indirect object often occurs after the prepositions *to* or *for*. Draw two lines under the indirect object.

B. Discuss your answers with the class and read the Form charts to check them.

▶ Verbs with Direct Objects

ONLINE PRACTICE

DIRECT OBJECTS		
SUBJECT	**VERB**	**DIRECT OBJECT**
People	make	**special food**.
Some people	send	**cards and gifts**.

▶ Verbs with Direct and Indirect Objects

DIRECT OBJECT + *TO/FOR* + INDIRECT OBJECT				
SUBJECT	**VERB**	**DIRECT OBJECT**	***TO/FOR***	**INDIRECT OBJECT**
People	send	**cards and gifts**	**to**	**them**.
	make	**special food**	**for**	**their friends**.

INDIRECT OBJECT + DIRECT OBJECT			
SUBJECT	**VERB**	**INDIRECT OBJECT**	**DIRECT OBJECT**
People	make	**their friends**	**special food.**
	send	**them**	**cards and gifts.**

Verbs with Direct Objects

- Some verbs have a direct object.
- A direct object is a person or a thing that receives the action of a verb. A direct object can be a noun or an object pronoun.
- A direct object follows a verb.

  Many people send **cards**.   Some people make **them**.

Verbs with Direct Objects and Indirect Objects

- Some verbs have two objects: a direct object and an indirect object.
- An indirect object is a person who receives the direct object. An indirect object can be a noun or an object pronoun.

Direct Object + To/For *+ Indirect Object*

- All verbs with both direct and indirect objects can follow this pattern: direct object + *to/for* + indirect object. In this pattern, the indirect object comes after the direct object. It follows *to* or *for*.

  I gave a book **to Irina**.   I cooked a meal **for Lee**.

- We can use this pattern with the verbs below.

To + **Indirect Object**				*For* + **Indirect Object**		
bring	mail	say	teach	bake	do	make
describe	offer	sell	tell	build	fix	prepare
explain	owe	send	write	buy	get	
give	repeat	show		cook	leave	

Indirect Object + Direct Object

- Some verbs with both direct and indirect objects can also follow this pattern: indirect object + direct object. In this pattern, the indirect object comes before the direct object, without the prepositions *to* or *for*.

  I cooked **Lee** a meal.   **x** I cooked for Lee a meal. (incorrect)

- We can use this pattern with the verbs below.

bake	bring	build	buy	cook	do	get	give	leave	mail
make	offer	owe	read	save	sell	send	show	tell	write

C1 Listening for Form

CD2 T35 **A. Listen to the sentences. Write the words or phrases you hear.**

_DO_ **1.** In China, people celebrate _Chinese New Year_ in January or February.

_____ **2.** They cook _____ delicious food.

_____ **3.** Some people also clean _____ before New Year's Eve.

_____ **4.** A lot of families hang _____ on the sides of the door.

_____ **5.** Many old people play _____ called "mahjiang."

_____ **6.** Adults give _____ red envelopes with money inside.

B. Look at your answers in part A. Write *DO* if your answer is a direct object and *IO* if your answer is an indirect object.

C2 Identifying Direct Objects

Read each sentence. Circle the direct object. Put an ✗ after the sentence if there is no direct object.

1. Brad joined (the army) four months ago.

2. He is very lonely.

3. He misses his friends and family a lot.

4. Last week Brad sent Carol a letter.

5. He asked her to marry him.

6. Carol was surprised.

7. Brad wants a wife.

8. Carol wants a career.

9. She is giving him an answer.

10. She is writing him a letter right now.

C3 Identifying Direct Objects and Indirect Objects

Read the letter. Look at the underlined words in each sentence. Write *DO* above the direct objects and *IO* above the indirect objects.

Dear Laura,

Last night I went to the Loy Krathong festival here in Thailand. Let me
describe *it* (1) for *you* (2). A krathong is a small boat. People make *them* (3)
from banana leaves. They put *a candle, incense, flowers, and coins* (4) in
the krathong. Then they put *the krathong* (5) into the river and make
a wish (6). My friend Somchai made *a krathong* (7) for *me* (8). After we left the
river, we went to a special meal. Somchai taught *me* (9) a special
Loy Krathong song (10).

Wish you were here,
Erica

C4 Forming Sentences with Direct and Indirect Objects

Form sentences with direct and indirect objects. Use the words and phrases.

1. Nancy/us/sent/a postcard/from Spain

   Nancy sent us a postcard from Spain.

2. bought/I/him/a present/yesterday

   _____

3. gave/her/a birthday cake/we

   _____

4. got/for/a glass of water/Mrs. Johnson/him

   _____

5. she/an essay/for/the school newspaper/wrote

   _____

6. they/photos/us/are showing/their

   _____

Direct Objects and Indirect Objects

Think Critically About Meaning and Use

A. Read the sentences and answer the questions below.

a. Greg bought a book for his teacher.

b. My boss announced his retirement to everyone this afternoon.

1. IDENTIFY Underline the direct objects and circle the indirect objects in the sentences.

2. ANALYZE Look at sentence a. What did Greg buy? Who received Greg's gift?

3. ANALYZE Look at sentence b. What did the boss announce? Who did he make the announcement to?

B. Discuss your answers with the class and read the Meaning and Use Notes to check them.

Meaning and Use Notes

ONLINE
PRACTICE

Direct Objects
▶ **1A** A direct object can be a person, place, or thing that a verb affects or changes in some way. It answers the questions *Who/Whom?* or *What?* A: <u>Who/Whom</u> did he see? B: He saw **his sister**. A: <u>What</u> is she explaining? B: She is explaining **her ideas**.
▶ **1B** Some verbs always have a direct object. Without an object, their meaning is not complete. Some common verbs that need direct objects are *bring, buy, get, have, like, make, need, say, take, turn on/off,* and *want.* Lynn **needs a car**. **x** Lynn needs. (incorrect)

Indirect Objects

▶ **2**   An indirect object is a person or group. It is the person that receives the direct object. It answers the questions *To whom?* and *For whom?* An indirect object can be an institution such as a library or a bank.

A: <u>To whom</u> did he send the check?   A: <u>For whom</u> did you buy a book?

B: Corey sent the check to **the bank**.   B: I bought a book **for Marta**.

Direct Object + *To/For* + Indirect Object vs. Indirect Object + Direct Object

▶ **3A**   There is no difference in meaning between direct object + *to/for* + indirect object and indirect object + direct object.

He is writing **a letter to us**. = He is writing **us a letter**.

She bought **a dress for me**. = She bought **me a dress**.

▶ **3B**   Some verbs have similar meanings but follow different patterns. For example, the verbs *say* and *tell* have similar meanings, but only *tell* can have an indirect object before a direct object.

Direct Object + *To/For* + Indirect Object	Indirect Object + Direct Object
He told **his name to the teacher**.	He told **the teacher his name**.
He said **his name to the teacher**.	**x** He said the teacher his name. (incorrect)

D1 Listening for Meaning and Use

▶ Notes 1A–3B

CD2 T36   Listen to the story about Sally. Is the word in the chart the direct object or the indirect object of the sentence? Check (✓) the correct column.

		DIRECT OBJECT	INDIRECT OBJECT
1.	Sally	✓	
2.	her		
3.	her		
4.	her		
5.	Sally		
6.	her		
7.	Sally		
8.	her		

D2 Using Direct Objects

▶ Notes 1A, 1B

Complete the sentences. Use direct objects.

1. I need _____ *a new car* _____ .

2. My town needs _____ .

3. I want _____ for my birthday.

4. Next year, I'm going to buy _____ .

5. My best friend has _____ .

6. I really like _____ .

D3 Using Indirect Objects

▶ Notes 2, 3A, 3B

Alexandra organized a picnic for her friend Amy's twenty-fifth birthday. Read her notes about things to do for the picnic. In your notebook, write full sentences to describe her preparations. Add an appropriate indirect object to each sentence.

1. send an email about the picnic

   Alexandra sent an email about the picnic to Amy's brother.

2. give directions

3. buy the food for the picnic

4. bake a chocolate cake

5. buy a birthday gift

6. write a short speech

D4 Talking About Holidays

▶ Notes 1A–3B

A. Answer the questions about a special holiday in your notebook. Use direct objects or indirect objects in your answers.

1. What special holiday do you celebrate every year?

   We celebrate Thanksgiving.

2. What foods do you cook?

3. What other things do you buy?

4. What other special things do you make?

5. What special clothes do you wear?

6. Who do you invite to celebrate with you?

B. Tell a partner about the holiday in part A. Use verbs such as *give, cook, bake,* and *make.* Use both sentence patterns for direct and indirect objects in your description.

People cook special treats on this day.
My aunt bakes pumpkin pie for the whole family.

Write About How a Classmate Celebrates His or Her Birthday

Think Critically About Meaning and Use

A. Complete each conversation.

1. A: Dan bought me a book for my birthday.

   B: _____

   a. Did you buy it for him?

   b. Was it good?

   c. Was it delicious?

2. A: They owe the bank a lot of money.

   B: _____

   a. They arrived yesterday.

   b. Did the bank pay them?

   c. That's terrible!

3. A: When did he speak to you about Mike's project?

   B: _____

   a. He talked to me last week.

   b. He worked on the project.

   c. He spoke to Mike.

4. A: Who taught you German?

   B: _____

   a. Ms. Werner taught me.

   b. I taught her.

   c. It did.

B. Discuss these questions in small groups.

1. **GENERATE** In 2, how would you rewrite speaker A's statement using the pattern: direct object + *to/for* + indirect object?

2. **IDENTIFY** In 4, what are the direct and indirect objects?

Edit

Some of these sentences have errors. Find the errors and correct them.

1. They explained the situation ^to^ us.

2. I made for you a cake.

3. He sends to us an email every month.

4. Frank's mother gave him the house.

5. We bought a bicycle my daughter.

6. He is cooking a meal for us.

7. They said me good-bye.

8. Let me tell she the answer.

Write

Write a paragraph about how a classmate celebrates his or her birthday. Use object pronouns, and direct and indirect objects.

1. **BRAINSTORM** Ask a classmate how he/she celebrates birthdays. Use these questions to make notes.
   - Does your family celebrate birthdays?
   - Are any birthdays more significant than others? Why?
   - Do you sing any special songs? What are they?
   - What special activities are there for birthdays?
   - Do you buy presents?
   - Do you eat any special foods on birthdays? What are they?

2. **WRITE A FIRST DRAFT** Before you write your first draft, read the checklist below. Write your draft using objects.

3. **EDIT** Read your work and check it against the checklist above. Circle grammar, spelling, and punctuation errors.

DO I ...	YES
include sentences with object pronouns?	☐
include sentences with direct and indirect objects?	☐
include some sentences with direct object + *to/for* + indirect object?	☐
include some sentences with indirect object + direct object?	☐
use the correct verb with indirect and/or direct objects?	☐

4. **PEER REVIEW** Work with a partner to help you decide how to fix your errors and improve the content.

5. **REWRITE YOUR DRAFT** Using the comments from your partner, write a final draft.

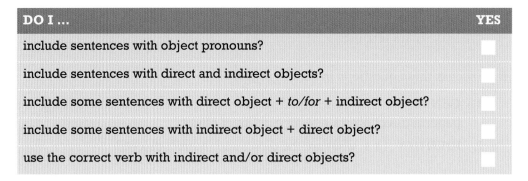

Marta's family celebrates her birthday every year. For her eighteenth birthday, they went to a restaurant and...

24

Infinitives and Gerunds After Verbs

Advice to Business Travelers

A1 Before You Read

Discuss these questions.

Is it important to be on time for work meetings? to meet friends?

A2 Read

 CD2 T37 Read the magazine article on the following page. What kinds of information should international business travelers find out about the country they will visit?

A3 After You Read

Linda Marsh went to Tokyo on business. Here are some of the things she did. According to the online article, were they mistakes or not? Check (✓) the correct column.

		MISTAKE	NOT A MISTAKE
1.	She didn't read about Japanese culture.	✓	
2.	She learned greetings in Japanese before she went.		
3.	She arrived the day before a national holiday.		
4.	She spoke to a Japanese colleague about working hours in Japan.		
5.	She was on time for her meeting.		
6.	She is friendly, so she called everyone by their first name.		

Advice to Business Travelers

International business travelers <u>need to know</u>
something about the customs of foreign countries.
Otherwise, the business trip may not be
successful. How do experienced business

5 travelers prepare for a trip to another country?
Many people like to talk to someone from the
country. Some people prefer to read about the
country. Others even learn to say a few simple
phrases in the native language of the country.

10 Business travel to a foreign country is always
difficult at first. But, according to experienced
business travelers, things begin to improve after a
few trips.

Here are a few helpful hints for any business trip abroad:

15 **Find out about office hours.**
When do your foreign colleagues start work each day? When do they like to eat lunch?
When do they finish working? What days do they work? You need to know these things
so you can schedule appointments at the right time.

Find out about religious and national holidays.
20 For example, experienced business travelers don't expect to do much business during
the week before and after Easter in countries like Italy and Spain. Employers and
employees around the world enjoy celebrating holidays. Do you need to travel to the
Middle East or Hong Kong? You probably don't want to plan a business trip during
Ramadan or the Chinese New Year. Check with someone from your host country
25 before you make final arrangements.

Find out about business customs.
In countries like Japan, business people expect to start meetings on time. In
other countries, people are more relaxed and they don't expect to start on time. In some
cultures, business people don't like discussing business at the start of a meeting. They
30 prefer beginning a discussion with small talk about the weather, art, or sports. There are
also different customs about names and titles, so avoid using first names immediately.

---

arrangements: plans, preparations
avoid: stay away from

experience: having the knowledge required for something
small talk: polite conversation about topics that are not
very serious

Infinitives and Gerunds After Verbs

Think Critically About Form

A. Look back at the article on page 361 and complete the tasks below.

1. **IDENTIFY** The underlined phrase is an example of a verb + infinitive. Find three more examples.

2. **APPLY** What two words form the infinitive?

3. **IDENTIFY** The circled phrase is an example of a verb + gerund. Find three more examples.

4. **EXPLAIN** How do we form the gerund?

B. Discuss your answers with the class and read the Form charts to check them.

ONLINE PRACTICE

VERB + INFINITIVE		
SUBJECT	**VERB**	**INFINITIVE**
I	need	
You	hope	**to work**.
She	decided	
They	wanted	

VERB + GERUND		
SUBJECT	**VERB**	**GERUND**
I	keep	
You	enjoy	**working**.
She	discussed	
They	finished	

VERB + INFINITIVE/GERUND		
SUBJECT	**VERB**	**INFINITIVE/GERUND**
I	like	
You	prefer	**to work**.
She	started	**working**.
They	began	

Verb + Infinitive

- To form the infinitive, add *to* to the base form of a verb.
- Infinitives can follow many verbs. For example:

decide	expect	hope	learn
need	plan	want	agree

Verb + Gerund

- To form the gerund, add *-ing* to the base form of a verb.
- Gerunds can follow many verbs. For example:

avoid	discuss	dislike	enjoy
finish	keep	practice	

Verb + Infinitive/Gerund

- We can use some verbs with either the gerund or the infinitive. For example:

begin	like	love	hate
prefer	start	try	

B1 Listening for Form

CD2 T38   **Listen to each sentence. Do you hear an infinitive or a gerund? Check (✓) the correct column.**

	INFINITIVE	GERUND
1.	✓	
2.		
3.		
4.		
5.		
6.		
7.		
8.		

B2 Identifying Infinitives and Gerunds

Read each sentence. If the sentence contains an infinitive, write *I*. If the sentence contains a gerund, write *G*. If it doesn't contain an infinitive or a gerund, write *X*.

_G_ **1.** Paula and Lisa enjoy playing tennis.

_____ **2.** Julia goes to class three days a week.

_____ **3.** My parents plan to buy a new car.

_____ **4.** She is learning to play the guitar.

_____ **5.** Juan wants to buy a new car.

_____ **6.** He really enjoys working with other people.

_____ **7.** She is learning Polish.

_____ **8.** Magda finished writing her dissertation last year.

B3 Building Sentences with Infinitives and Gerunds

A. Build two affirmative and two negative statements with a verb + infinitive. Use each word or phrase only once. Make any changes necessary to the verbs in the second and third columns. Punctuate your sentences correctly.

the students	want	pass this course
her boss	need	speak Chinese
our teacher	learn	sign the contract
his parents	plan	move to California

The students want to pass this course.

B. Build two affirmative and two negative statements with a verb + gerund. Use each word or phrase only once. Make any changes necessary to the verbs in the second and third columns. Punctuate your sentences correctly.

most of my friends	enjoy	take piano lessons last year
my cousin and I	keep	speak in front of a large audience
Philip	discuss	make mistakes
I	avoid	open a business together

Most of my friends enjoyed taking piano lessons last year.

B4 Forming Questions with Infinitives and Gerunds

A. Form questions with a verb + infinitive or a verb + gerund. Use the words and phrases. Punctuate your sentences correctly.

1. What/do/you/plan/do/this evening

   What do you plan to do this evening?

2. What/do/you/want/do/this summer

3. Where/do/your/friends/enjoy/go/on/weekends

4. What kinds of/films/do/you/avoid/watch

5. What/do/you/hope/do/in the future

6. Where/do/you/expect/live/in ten years

 B. Work with a partner. Take turns asking and answering the questions in part A.

   A: What do you plan to do this evening?
   B: I plan to go to that new restaurant on Smith Street.

B5 Choosing the Infinitive or the Gerund

Choose the correct form. In some cases both answers are possible.

1. I like _____ cakes.

   a. to bake
   b. baking

2. Paul enjoys _____ to classical music.

   a. to listen
   b. listening

3. Pat is finally learning _____ .

   a. to drive
   b. driving

4. Lee prefers _____ slowly.

   a. to work
   b. working

5. She needs _____ harder.

   a. to work
   b. working

6. Maria started _____ more carefully after the accident.

   a. to drive
   b. driving

7. At the meeting, we discussed _____ a new employee.

   a. to hire
   b. hiring

8. At the age of 60, she began _____ the piano.

   a. to learn
   b. learning

C MEANING AND USE

Infinitives and Gerunds

Think Critically About Meaning and Use

A. Read the sentences and answer the questions below.

a. We like Mexican food.　　　　**c.** We like to eat Mexican food.
b. We like eating Mexican food.

1. **ANALYZE** Which sentences talk about an activity? Which sentence does not?

2. **COMPARE AND CONTRAST** Which two sentences have exactly the same meaning?

B. Discuss your answers with the class and read the Meaning and Use Notes to check them.

Meaning and Use Notes

ONLINE PRACTICE

Referring to Activities and States

▶ **1A** We use infinitives and gerunds to refer to activities or states. We can use them in the same position in the sentence as a direct object.

Activities	States
He <u>loves</u> **tennis**.	They <u>hate</u> **cold weather**.
He <u>loves</u> **to play** tennis.	They <u>hate</u> **to be** cold.
He <u>loves</u> **playing** tennis.	They <u>hate</u> **being** cold.

▶ **1B** After the verbs *like, hate, love, prefer, begin,* and *start,* we can use an infinitive or a gerund with little or no difference in meaning.

I <u>like</u> **to travel** alone. = I <u>like</u> traveling alone.　　She <u>started</u> **to leave**. = She <u>started</u> **leaving**.

They <u>prefer</u> **to walk**. = They <u>prefer</u> walking.　　It <u>began</u> **to rain**. = It <u>began</u> **raining**.

Expressing Likes and Dislikes

▶ **2** We often use verbs with infinitives and gerunds to discuss our like or dislike of an activity or state.

I <u>enjoy</u> **cooking**, but I <u>dislike</u> **cleaning**.　　We <u>love</u> **to ski**.

Marta <u>loves</u> **being** healthy and <u>hates</u> **being** sick.　　They <u>hate</u> **to be** late.

C1 Listening for Meaning and Use ▶ Notes 1A–2

CD2 T39 Listen to the sentences. Choose the sentence that has the same meaning as the one you hear.

1. **a.** Susan hates her house.

   b. Susan hates cleaning her house. *(circled)*

2. **a.** Josh dislikes sleeping late.

   b. Josh likes sleeping late.

3. **a.** Holly didn't enjoy the movie.

   b. Holly doesn't like to go to movies.

4. **a.** Rob dislikes working on Saturdays.

   b. Rob prefers to work on Mondays.

5. **a.** We decided to work late.

   b. We don't like to work late.

6. **a.** Derek dislikes taking tests.

   b. Derek prefers taking tests.

C2 Talking About Activities and States ▶ Notes 1A–2

A. Complete each sentence with a gerund or infinitive. Use an appropriate form of one of the phrases below or use your own ideas.

be a vegetarian	clean my room	jog in the park	study for exams
borrow money	eat red meat	shop for clothes	take a vacation

1. I hate _____ *cleaning my room* _____.

2. I always avoid _____.

3. Next month I expect _____.

4. Last summer I enjoyed _____.

5. As a child, I avoided _____.

6. A few months ago I really needed _____.

7. I strongly dislike _____.

8. Last year I decided _____.

B. Work in small groups. Share your answers to part A. Discuss the structures you used.

1. In which sentences can you use only a gerund?

2. In which sentences can you use only an infinitive?

3. In which sentences can you use either a gerund or an infinitive?

C3 Expressing Likes and Dislikes

▶ Notes 1A–2

A. **Answer the questions with complete sentences in your notebook. Use gerunds or infinitives in your answers.**

1. What two things do you enjoy doing on Sunday?

   On Sunday I enjoy riding my bicycle and playing tennis.

2. What holiday do you love to celebrate? What two things do you like to do on this day?

3. What three things do you enjoy doing after a stressful day?

4. What two household chores do you dislike doing?

5. What three things do you want to do in the near future?

6. What two things did you love to do as a child?

7. What two things did you hate doing as a child?

8. What three things do you want to do in the next year?

 B. **Work with a partner. Take turns asking and answering the questions in part A. Use the chart to take notes on your partner's answers.**

1.	likes sleeping late, going for long walks, renting DVDs
2.	loves to celebrate Thanksgiving…
3.	
4.	
5.	
6.	
7.	
8.	

 C. **Exchange partners. Tell you new partner about your first partner's answers.**

On Sunday Ana enjoys sleeping late, going for long walks, and renting DVDs.

Think Critically About Meaning and Use

A. Complete each conversation.

1. A: Do you like making cookies?

B: _____

   a. No, but I like to eat them.

   b. I like chocolate cookies.

   c. No, I don't like them.

2. A: Do you go to a gym?

B: _____

   a. No, I like to exercise.

   b. No, I dislike exercising.

   c. No, the gym is new.

3. A: He quit his job last week.

B: _____

   a. Did he dislike working there?

   b. Does he like to leave?

   c. Does he enjoy working there?

4. A: Do you avoid taking the train?

B: _____

   a. No, I don't like to take the train.

   b. Yes, I like to take the train.

   c. No, I like taking the train.

B. Discuss these questions in small groups.

1. **EVALUATE** In 1, does the meaning of the answer change if speaker B says: "No, but I like eating them?"

2. **PREDICT** In the answer to 2, can we replace the gerund with an infinitive? Why or why not?

Edit

Find the errors in this paragraph and correct them.

   Keisha plans ~~going~~ *to go* to college next year, so she is starting apply to different schools. She wants to go to a school in Chicago because she wants live at home. In this way, she'll avoid to spending a lot of money on room and board. She enjoys to study biology and chemistry, and she likes help people. She wants to becoming a nurse. Her grades are good so she expects get into several schools in the area.

Write

Write a paragraph with advice for business travelers visiting your country for the first time. Use verbs with infinitives and gerunds.

1. **BRAINSTORM** Think about how people in your country expect to do business. Use these questions to help you.

   - Do business people expect others to be on time?
   - Do they prefer to use first names or formal titles?
   - When do they avoid doing business?
   - What do people in your country expect visitors to do?
   - Do people in your country expect visitors to bring a gift when invited for dinner?
   - Should visitors avoid doing certain things in a person's home?

2. **WRITE A FIRST DRAFT** Before you write your first draft, read the checklist below and look at the example on page 361. Write your draft using infinitives and gerunds.

3. **EDIT** Read your work and check it against the checklist below. Circle grammar, spelling, and punctuation errors.

DO I ...	YES
use infinitives after verbs?	☐
use gerunds after verbs?	☐
include infinitives and gerunds that refer to activities and states?	☐
include infinitives and gerunds that express likes and dislikes?	☐
include infinitives and gerunds that explain customs and habits?	☐

4. **PEER REVIEW** Work with a partner to help you decide how to fix your errors and improve the content.

5. **REWRITE YOUR DRAFT** Using the comments from your partner, write a final draft.

> Business customs in Japan are very formal. For example, business people bow to each other and they prefer calling their business associates by their last names...

Choose the correct word or words to complete each sentence.

1. Lynn offered _____ a piece of cake.

    a. to me   **c.** me

    b. for me   **d.** myself

2. Did they sell _____?

    a. to the piano   **c.** for the piano

    b. the piano Pete   **d.** Pete the piano

3. Please explain _____.

    a. the problem to us   **c.** us the problem

    b. for us the problem   **d.** the problem on us

4. I couldn't avoid _____ the teacher's question.

    a. say   **c.** to ask

    b. saying   **d.** answering

5. What kind of movies do you enjoy _____?

    a. to look   **c.** to see

    b. watching   **d.** looking

6. Yuki hates _____ her parents.

    a. to disappoint   **c.** to disappointing

    b. disappoint   **d.** disappointed

7. I forgot my wallet. Can you lend _____ some money?

    a. for me   **c.** me to

    b. to me   **d.** me

8. She expects _____ from the university soon.

    a. hearing   **c.** hears

    b. to hear   **d.** heard

9. He dislikes _____ in the city.

    a. driving   **c.** driven

    b. to drive   **d.** drives

Choose the correct response to complete each conversation.

10. **A:** Do you usually drive to New York?

    B: _____

        a. Actually, I drive to New York.

        b. Yes, I decided to drive this time.

        c. No, I decided to fly.

        d. Actually, I prefer to fly.

11. **A:** My brother likes to wake up early.

    B: _____

        a. I am, too.

        b. Yes, I do.

        c. I don't. I prefer sleeping late.

        d. I wake up, too.

12. **A:** Do you avoid taking the train?

    B: _____

        a. No, I don't like to take the train.

        b. Yes, I like to take the train.

        c. No, I like taking the train.

        d. Yes, I take the train.

13. **A:** I like to play tennis.

    B: _____

        a. I dislike it, too.

        b. I prefer to swim.

        c. Do you avoid it?

        d. I dislike avoiding it.

14. **A:** Did you discuss the problem?

    B: No. _____

        a. We kept talking about it.

        b. We began to talk about it.

        c. We avoided talking about it.

        d. We prefer talking about it.

Match the response to the question below.

15. Who's the postcard for?

16. What did she tell them?

17. Who gave it to her?

18. Who did she give them to?

19. What are you sending them?

20. Did he speak to her?

    a. I sent them to Mike.

    b. Some clothes.

    c. To her mother.

    d. For my brother.

    e. I did.

    g. Yes, he did.

    f. A lie.

CHAPTER

25

Comparatives

Smartphones

A1 Before You Read

 Discuss these questions.

Do you own a cell phone? What kind of cell phone do you own? Besides making phone calls, what special things can your cell phone do?

A2 Read

 CD2 T40 Read the online article about smartphones on the following page. How many kinds of cell phones are there? What kinds of things can a traditional feature cell phone do? What kinds of things can a smartphone do?

A3 After You Read

Read the statements. Check (✓) the correct column.

		FEATURE PHONE	SMARTPHONE
1.	This phone is more popular.	✓	
2.	Many people still buy this phone.		
3.	This phone can download and run programs more efficiently.		
4.	This phone has more advanced computing ability.		
5.	This phone is more popular with consumers 24 to 35 years old.		
6.	The technology for this phone is older.		

Smartphones

These days, almost everyone carries a cell phone. Cell phone technology is improving quickly in the 21st century, and the range of cell phones is greater
5 than in the past. There are two basic kinds of cell phones: "feature phones" and "smartphones."

The older feature phones are cell phones with a number of important tools.
10 These include text messaging, a calendar, a contact list, a digital camera, and voice recording. And, of course, feature phones also have the ability to make and receive phone calls.

15 In contrast, the newer smartphones have all the features of a traditional feature phone plus many others. These include GPS, a high-quality digital camera, Wi-Fi, and the ability to send
20 and receive information over the Internet. In general, programs for smartphones run faster than feature-phone programs. They also allow users to install a wide range of useful applications. Another
25 improvement is that cell phone signals for smartphones are often stronger than the signals for older phones.

In the earlier days of smartphones, users had to use a "stylus" to write in
30 and then point to the phone numbers they wanted to call. Users had to work harder to make things happen, and things happened more slowly. Today, they simply touch the screen to dial a
35 number. Smartphones were also more expensive in the earlier days. Today, consumers can buy smartphones more cheaply than in the past.

Overall, smartphones are faster,
40 more efficient, and "smarter" than feature phones, but feature phones are still more popular with many groups of consumers. Consumers between the ages of 24 and 35, however, are more likely to buy
45 smartphones. In this age group, the number of smartphone users is bigger now than it was in the past. If prices continue to go down, smartphones will become more popular for all age groups.

---

application: a specialized computer program

GPS: Global Positioning System (a system that uses satellite signals to help users find places)

signal: energy wave that enables phones to make and receive calls and connect to the Internet

stylus: a pen-like tool used to write on a phone or computer screen

Wi-Fi: Wireless Fidelity (a system that allows users to send and receive information over wireless networks)

B FORM

The Comparative with Adjectives and Adverbs

Think Critically About Form

A. Look back at the article on page 375 and complete the tasks below.

1. **APPLY** Look at the circled words. These are the comparative forms of the adjectives and adverbs below. Write the comparative form next to each adjective or adverb below. How do we form the comparatives of these words?

   Adjectives   *Adverbs*

   great _____   fast _____

   old _____   hard _____

2. **APPLY** Look at the underlined phrases. These are the comparative forms of the adjectives and adverbs below. Write the comparative form next to each adjective or adverb below. How do we form the comparatives of these words?

   Adjectives   *Adverb*

   expensive _____   slowly _____

   efficient _____   cheaply _____

B. Discuss your answers with the class and read the Form charts to check them.

▶ Regular Comparative Forms

ONLINE PRACTICE

ONE-SYLLABLE ADJECTIVES	
ADJECTIVE	COMPARATIVE
big	**bigger**
strong	**stronger**
young	**younger**

TWO-SYLLABLE ADJECTIVES	
ADJECTIVE	COMPARATIVE
simple	**simpler**
easy	**easier**
famous	**more famous**

THREE-SYLLABLE ADJECTIVES	
ADJECTIVE	COMPARATIVE
efficient	**more efficient**
popular	**more popular**

ONE-SYLLABLE ADVERBS	
ADVERB	COMPARATIVE
fast	**faster**
hard	**harder**

TWO- OR THREE-SYLLABLE ADVERBS	
ADVERB	COMPARATIVE
slowly	**more slowly**
frequently	**more frequently**

Adjectives with One Syllable

- Add *-er* to form the comparative. If the adjective ends in *-e*, add *-r*.
- For adjectives that end with a single vowel and a consonant, double the final consonant and add *-er*.

Adjectives with Two Syllables

- Some two-syllable adjectives use *-er*. Other two-syllable adjectives use either *-er* or *more*. See Appendix 10 for adjectives that use both forms of the comparative.

    Jenny is **friendlier/more friendly** than her sister.

- If an adjective ends in a consonant + *-y*, change the *y* to *i* and add *-er*.

Adjectives with Three or More Syllables

- Use *more* with adjectives of three or more syllables.

Adverbs with One Syllable

- Add *-er* to form the comparative.

Adverbs with Two or More Syllables

- For adverbs of two or more syllables ending in *-ly*, use *more* instead of *-er*.

▶ Irregular Comparative Forms

ADJECTIVE	ADVERB	COMPARATIVE	ADJECTIVE	ADVERB	COMPARATIVE
good	well	**better**	bad	badly	**worse**

▶ The Comparative In Sentences

	COMPARATIVE	*THAN*	SUBJECT (+ VERB or AUXILIARY)
A mile is	**longer**		a kilometer.
Vanilla ice cream is	**more popular**	**than**	chocolate ice cream is.
Chris drives	**faster**		Gloria drives.
My grandfather talks	**more slowly**		my father does.

- Use the comparative form of an adjective or adverb + *than*.
- Use *than* to connect the two parts of a comparative sentence.
- We sometimes use the main verb or an auxiliary verb *(be, do)* in the second part of a comparative sentence.

B1 Listening for Form

🔊 CD2 T41　Listen to each sentence. What comparative form do you hear? Check (✓) the correct column.

	REGULAR FORM WITH -ER	REGULAR FORM WITH MORE	IRREGULAR FORM
1.	✓		
2.			
3.			
4.			
5.			
6.			
7.			
8.			

B2 Forming Comparatives

A. Write the comparative form of the adjectives and adverbs.

Adjectives

1. thin ___thinner___
2. easy _____
3. intelligent _____
4. expensive _____

Adverbs

5. fast _____
6. happily _____
7. quietly _____
8. carefully _____

B. Write the base form of the comparative adjectives and adverbs.

Adjectives

1. bigger ___big___
2. nicer _____
3. taller _____
4. prettier _____

Adverbs

5. worse _____
6. better _____
7. more slowly _____
8. more efficiently _____

B3 Making Comparative Statements

Complete the statements. Use the comparative form of the adjectives and adverbs in parentheses.

1. Color printers are __more expensive than__ (expensive) black-and-white printers.

2. Uploading a document on the Internet is _____ (fast) mailing a document.

3. Email works _____ (quickly) regular mail.

4. Desktop computers are _____ (big) laptops, but laptops are _____ (light) desktop computers.

5. Cell phones are _____ (convenient) regular phones, but regular phones are _____ (reliable) cell phones.

6. Computers can solve some problems _____ (fast) and _____ (accurately) humans.

B4 Working on Comparative Adjectives and Adverbs

Complete the conversations. Use the comparative form of the adjectives and adverbs in parentheses.

Conversation 1

Hiro: Let's rent the movie *The Incredibles*.

Yuki: I want to see something __more serious__ (serious). How about
$\overline{}_{1}$
Gone with the Wind?

Hiro: It's too long! I'll fall asleep. What about *Pirates of the Carribean*? It's
$\underline{}_{2}$ (short).

Yuki: But it's a lot $\underline{}_{3}$ (violent).

Hiro: I know. Let's rent both, and we'll see which one is $\underline{}_{4}$ (enjoyable).

Conversation 2

Elena: Lee should be the new manager. He works $\underline{}_{1}$ (hard) than Rick.

Andre: Well, Lee supervises $\underline{}_{2}$ (effectively) than Rick does, but Rick is
$\underline{}_{3}$ (friendly). Everyone likes him.

Elena: I agree that Rick is $\underline{}_{4}$ (popular), but can he do a
$\underline{}_{5}$ (good) job than Lee does?

C MEANING AND USE

Making Comparisons

 Think Critically About Meaning and Use

A. Read the sentences and answer the questions below.

a. Ruth and Susan are sisters. Ruth is younger.
b. George drives more slowly than Meg.
c. My car is newer than Lee's car.

1. EVALUATE Which sentence compares people?

2. EVALUATE Which sentence compares things?

3. EVALUATE Which sentence compares actions?

B. Discuss your answers with the class and read the Meaning and Use Notes to check them.

Meaning and Use Notes

ONLINE PRACTICE

Comparing People, Things, or Actions
▶ **1A** We use comparatives to talk about the differences between people, things, or actions. We often use comparatives to express opinions.   Holly is **taller than** Carl. Paris is **more beautiful than** Rome.   Buses are **slower than** trains. Joanna dances **more gracefully than** Laura.
▶ **1B** *Less* is the opposite of *more*.   Computers are **less expensive** than they were ten years ago. Computers are **more efficient** than they were ten years ago.
▶ **1C** We do not always use a phrase or a clause with *than* to make a comparison in every sentence. Often, the second part of the sentence with *than* is not necessary in the context.   Smartphones are **smaller than** laptops. They are much **more efficient,** too. They are **faster,** and they're **more convenient** to use.

C1 Listening for Meaning and Use

▶ Notes 1A–1C

 CD1 T42 Listen to the information. Choose the correct answer for each question.

1. **a.** Yes.
   b. No.

2. **a.** Tyrone.
   b. Tamika.

3. **a.** Jack.
   b. Paul.

4. **a.** Brad.
   b. Sasha.

5. **a.** A sports car.
   b. An SUV.

6. **a.** Keiko.
   b. Koji.

7. **a.** Mr. Ryan's.
   b. Mr. Larkin's.

8. **a.** A computer.
   b. A smartphone.

C2 Making Comparisons

▶ Notes 1A–1C

Work with a partner. Compare the people or things in the pictures. Use the adjectives and adverbs below or others of your choice. Use *more* or *less*. Make as many sentences as you can.

dangerous	fast	noisy	slow	useful	quiet
exciting	high	safe	strong	well	beautiful

1a. _A bicycle is safer_ _____

2a. _____

3a. _____

1b. _____

2b. _____

3b. _____

C3 Expressing Similarities and Differences

▶ Notes 1A–1C

A. Choose three of the categories below. Think of two things or people to compare in each category. Write at least three comparisons for each in your notebook. Use adjectives and adverbs. Try to alternate the subjects in your sentences.

airports	cities	kinds of food	styles of music
athletes	holidays	members of your family	TV shows

Classical music is calmer and more restful than rock music. Rock music is...

 B. Work with a partner. Share your comparisons.

C4 Expressing Opinions

▶ Notes 1A–1C

A. Read the two paragraphs. What is Paragraph 1 about? What is Paragraph 2 about?

Paragraph 1

Modern technology is bringing people together. We now have cell phones, webcams, and instant chat forums on the Internet. Calling people in other places is much less expensive than it was just a few years ago. And email is faster than regular mail and cheaper than a telephone call. With these inventions it's easy to communicate frequently with our friends, our family, and the whole world.

Paragraph 2

People don't communicate in the world today. First, TV replaced family time. Instead of talking together, people started sitting quietly in front of the TV. Now, we have the Internet. People talk to strangers, but they don't talk to the people in their own homes! We need to communicate more effectively with our own families.

 B. Work with a partner. Share your comparisons.

1. Which paragraph do you agree with? Why?

   I agree with paragraph 1. Technology is bringing people together because...

2. How is communication different today compared to the past?

3. Is life better today, or was it better before? Why?

Think Critically About Meaning and Use

A. Complete each conversation.

1. A: He's taller than everyone in his class.

B: _____

a. Is he taller than his father, too?

b. Don't worry. He'll grow soon.

c. Is he shorter than his friends?

2. A: You're smarter than Paul.

B: _____

a. Then why are my grades worse?

b. You're always criticizing me.

c. Yes, you are.

3. A: Soo-jin is much more responsible than she was before.

B: _____

a. Her boss is going to make her a manager.

b. That's too bad.

c. She never comes to work on time.

4. A: Jason was sick yesterday, and he's worse today.

B: _____

a. We should call the doctor.

b. Then he can go to work.

c. That's great!

B. Discuss these questions in small groups.

1. **DRAW A CONCLUSION** Look at 2. What is true about Paul? (Complete the statements.)

a. Paul is _____ intelligent than speaker B.

b. Paul's grades are _____ than speaker B's grades.

2. **PREDICT** In 4, what is the answer if A says: "Paul was sick yesterday, but he's better today."?

Edit

Some of these sentences have errors. Find the errors and correct them.

1. Carl is a ~~good~~ *better* student than you are.

2. Davis High School is large than Union High School.

3. Who is more tall?

4. Ling sings beautifully than Sam.

5. My new teacher is nicer than my old teacher.

6. Erica is friendlier from Luiz.

7. My shoes are more newer than yours.

8. Is Mike more efficient than Anna?

Write

Write a paragraph comparing two people that you know. Use comparative adjectives and adverbs.

1. **BRAINSTORM** Think of two people you know. List all their similarities and differences. Use these instructions to help you.
   - Describe the two people's appearances.
   - Describe their personalities.
   - Talk about their actions.
   - Talk about their hobbies.
   - List some information about things they own.
   - Describe how you feel about them.

2. **WRITE A FIRST DRAFT** Before you write your first draft, read the checklist below. Write your draft using comparatives.

3. **EDIT** Read your work and check it against the checklist below. Circle grammar, spelling, and punctuation errors.

DO I ...	YES
use the comparative with adjectives?	☐
use the comparative with adverbs?	☐
include regular comparative forms of one, two, and three or more syllables?	☐
include at least two irregular comparative forms?	☐
make comparisons about people?	☐
make comparisons about things?	☐
make comparisons about actions?	☐

4. **PEER REVIEW** Work with a partner to help you decide how to fix your errors and improve the content.

5. **REWRITE YOUR DRAFT** Using the comments from your partner, write a final draft.

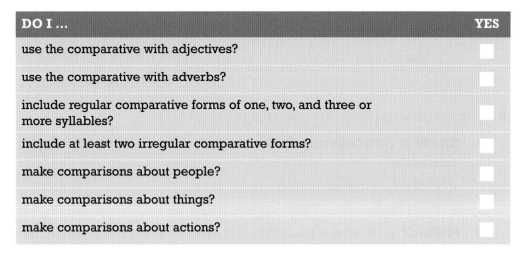

I have two younger brothers, Steve and Jeff. Steve is younger than Jeff, but Steve is taller...

26

Superlatives

The Greatest Invention Since Sliced Bread

A1 Before You Read

Discuss these questions.

How many inventions can you think of? How many inventors can you think of? What are the most important inventions of all time?

A2 Read

 CD2 T43 Read the online newspaper article on the following page. What interesting facts can you relate about the following inventions: sliced bread, sandwiches, children's toys, ATMs?

A3 After You Read

Write the name of the invention in the space provided.

	INVENTION THAT IS FAMOUS FOR ...	NAME OF INVENTION
1.	The most loved board game	
2.	The most popular doll	
3.	The fastest way to get money from a bank	
4.	The most amazing invention of the 20th century	
5.	The most useful invention for people who make mistakes	
6.	An invention that makes the world smaller	

The Greatest Inventions Since Sliced Bread?

In 1928, Otto Rohwedder of Iowa invented the first machine for slicing and wrapping bread. It was a very important invention, and is still the most efficient way to commercially slice bread. Since then, people often talk about new inventions as being "the greatest thing since sliced bread." In fact, history tells us that sliced bread existed well before 1928. In 1762, the 4th Earl of Sandwich was too busy to sit down to a real meal so he asked his cook to bring him some cold meat between two "slices" of bread. The snack became fashionable, and the "sandwich" was born! So in fact it was Rohwedder's slicing machine (and not sliced bread itself) in 1928 that gave us the phrase.

Since then, there have been plenty of inventions: some serious and world-changing, and some not so serious but still influential. One influential but not so serious invention is Monopoly (1936). Monopoly is one of the most loved board games of modern times. Another is Barbie (1956), the most popular doll of all times. A third is liquid paper (1951), the most useful for those of us who make mistakes. But these are hardly "the greatest thing since sliced bread." So what are?

The ATM (short for "Automated Teller Machine"), invented in 1939, is the fastest and easiest way to get money from a bank. The computer (1936) is, without a doubt, the most amazing invention of the 20th century. Satellite technology (1957) is a great invention that makes the world smaller, and the microchip (1959) is a small invention that makes a big difference to the lives of people all over the world. These and other modern inventions are indeed better than sliced bread!

What will the newest version of "the greatest thing since sliced bread" be? It's hard to say, but keep watching the world around you. Great things are being invented every day!

---

influential: important and powerful
slice: to cut into pieces

wrap: to cover something in paper or plastic

B FORM

The Superlative with Adjectives and Adverbs

Think Critically About Form

A. Look back at the article on page 387 and complete the tasks below.

1. **APPLY** Look at the underlined phrases. These are superlative forms of the adjective and adverb below. Write the superlative form next to the adjective and adverb below. How do we form the superlative of these words?

   Adjective   *Adverb*

   great _____   fast _____

2. **APPLY** Look at the circled phrases. These are the superlative forms of the adjectives below. Write the superlative form next to the adjectives below. How do we form the superlative of these words?

   popular _____   efficient _____

   useful _____

B. Discuss your answers with the class and read the Form charts to check them.

▶ Regular Superlative Forms

ONLINE
PRACTICE

ONE-SYLLABLE ADJECTIVES		
ADJECTIVE	COMPARATIVE	SUPERLATIVE
old	older	**the oldest**
weak	weaker	**the weakest**
big	bigger	**the biggest**

TWO-SYLLABLE ADJECTIVES		
ADJECTIVE	COMPARATIVE	SUPERLATIVE
simple	simpler	**the simplest**
easy	easier	**the easiest**
famous	more famous	**the most famous**

THREE-SYLLABLE ADJECTIVES		
ADJECTIVE	COMPARATIVE	SUPERLATIVE
efficient	more efficient	**the most efficient**
popular	more popular	**the most popular**

ONE-SYLLABLE ADVERBS		
ADVERB	COMPARATIVE	SUPERLATIVE
fast	faster	**the fastest**
hard	harder	**the hardest**

TWO- OR THREE-SYLLABLE ADVERBS		
ADVERB	COMPARATIVE	SUPERLATIVE
slowly	more slowly	**the most slowly**
frequently	more frequently	**the most frequently**

Adjectives with One Syllable

- To form the superlative, use *the* + adjective + *-est*.
- For adjectives that end with a single vowel and a consonant, double the final consonant and add *-est*.

Adjectives with Two Syllables

- Some two-syllable adjectives add *-est*. Some two-syllable adjectives add *the most*. See Appendix 10 for adjectives that use both forms of the superlative.

    John is **the friendliest / the most friendly**.

- If an adjective ends in a consonant + *-y*, change the *y* to *i* and add *-est*.

Adjectives with Three or More Syllables

- Use *the most* with adjectives of three or more syllables.

Adverbs with One Syllable

- Add *-est* to form the superlative.

Adverbs with Two or More Syllables

- Use *the most* with adverbs of two or more syllables.

▶ Irregular Superlative Forms

ADJECTIVE	ADVERB	SUPERLATIVE
good	well	**the best**
bad	badly	**the worst**

▶ The Superlative In Sentences

	SUPERLATIVE	
Tom is	**the tallest**	student in the class.
Kim speaks	**the most fluently**	of all the students.

(Continued on page 390)

> Do not use *than* after superlatives. Use prepositional phrases such as *in the* ... and ... *of all*.
>
> They are the most important inventions **in the world**.
>
> They are the most important inventions **of all**.
>
> **X** They are the most important inventions than all. (incorrect)

B1 Listening for Form

CD2 T44 Listen to each sentence. Do you hear a comparative or a superlative? Check (✓) the correct column.

	COMPARATIVE	SUPERLATIVE
1.		✓
2.		
3.		
4.		
5.		
6.		
7.		
8.		

B2 Forming Superlatives

A. Write the superlative form of the adjectives and adverbs.

Adjectives

1. tall   _the tallest_
2. easy   _____
3. intelligent _____
4. new   _____

Adverbs

5. happily   _____
6. gracefully _____
7. fluently   _____
8. carefully _____

B. Write the base form of the comparative adjectives and adverbs.

Adjectives   *Adverbs*

1. the biggest _____big_____   5. the fastest _____

2. the prettiest _____   6. the worst _____

3. the thinnest _____   7. the most quickly _____

4. the happiest _____   8. the best _____

B3 Working with Superlative Adjectives and Adverbs

Complete the conversations. Use the superlative form of the adjectives and adverbs in parentheses.

Conversation 1

A: How's Dan doing in your Latin class? He says that he's _____the worst_____ (bad)
    ₁
in the class.

B: Nonsense! He should get the _____ (high) grade. He works
                    ₂
_____ (hard).
        ₃

Conversation 2

A: I'm going to fire Linda. She is _____ (careless) of all my employees.
                        ₁

B: Who are _____ (good) workers?
            ₂

A: Derek and Ruth work _____ (efficiently).
                    ₃

Conversation 3

A: Who is _____ (bad) driver in your family?
        ₁

B: My older sister. She's terrible. My younger sister drives the _____
                                ₂
(carefully).

Conversation 4

A: What is _____ (long) river in the world?
        ₁

B: I think it's the Nile in Africa. But the Amazon in South America carries
_____ (large) volume of water.
        ₂

C MEANING AND USE

Superlatives

Think Critically About Meaning and Use

A. Read the sentences and answer the questions below.

   a. Dan walks faster than Rick.
   b. Dan is slower than Bob.
   c. Bob walks the fastest of the three. Rick walks the slowest.

   1. EVALUATE Which sentence compares two actions?

   2. EVALUATE Which compares two people?

   3. INTERPRET Which sentences show that something is first or last in a group of three or more?

B. Discuss your answers with the class and read the Meaning and Use Notes to check them.

Meaning and Use Notes

ONLINE PRACTICE

Comparing Three or More People, Things, or Actions
▶ **1A**   We use superlatives to compare people, things, or actions in a group of three or more. We often use superlatives to express opinions.   Hong Kong is **the most expensive** place to live.   Kyoto is **the most beautiful** city in Japan.
▶ **1B**   *Least* is the opposite of *most*.   Ferraris are **the most expensive** cars in the world. Fords are **the least expensive**.   My math class is **the least interesting** of all my classes this semester.
▶ **1C**   We do not always use an expression with *in* or *of* in sentences with superlatives. Often it is not necessary in the context.   Sam is **the tallest** <u>in the family</u>. John is **the shortest** and Ana is **the most intelligent**.

C1 Listening for Meaning and Use

▶ Notes 1A–1C

(( )) CD2 T45 Listen to the conversation. Check (✓) the school that is the best in each category.

		LIGHTHOUSE UNIVERSITY	WESTBROOK COLLEGE	CRANBERRY UNIVERSITY
1.	reputation	✓		
2.	cheap			
3.	close to home			
4.	easy to get in			
5.	comfortable dorms			
6.	famous professors			
7.	friendly students			
8.	beautiful campus			

C2 Expressing Opinions

▶ Notes 1A–1C

A. There are many different ways to compare languages. Write sentences using the notes below. Use superlatives to describe which language is first or last in each category.

1. easy to learn ___Spanish is the easiest to learn._____

2. hard to read _____

3. useful for business _____

4. easy spelling rules _____

5. simple grammar _____

6. difficult pronunciation _____

B. Discuss your opinions in small groups. Do you agree?

C3 Making Comparisons

▶ Notes 1A–1C

A. Work with a partner. Make guesses about the animals below. Match each of the animals to one of the world records.

anaconda	blue whale	hummingbird	sea turtle
bar-headed goose	cheetah	peregrine falcon	sea wasp jellyfish

	ANIMALS	WORLD RECORDS
1.	hummingbird	Some of these birds are only 2 inches long.
2.		This bird can dive at speeds of 270 miles per hour.
3.		This snake can grow to a length of 30 feet.
4.		This animal can reach a speed of 70 miles per hour.
5.		This animal can weigh up to 30 tons.
6.		This sea animal is 30 times more deadly than a cobra.
7.		This sea animal can live to 200 years.
8.		This bird can fly above 29,000 feet.

B. Now see Appendix 12 to check your answers. How many right answers do you have?

C. Write a statement in your notebook about each animal using a superlative adjective or adverb.

The hummingbird is the smallest bird in the world.

C4 Expressing Opinions

▶ Notes 1A–1C

Make one comparative and one superlative statement about each category below. Use the adjectives in parentheses. Use *the least* and *the most* in some of your statements. Discuss your answers with a partner.

1. **ice cream flavors (delicious):**   chocolate   vanilla   strawberry

   Vanilla ice cream is more delicious than strawberry.
   Chocolate is the most delicious ice cream flavor of all.

2. **cities (expensive):**   Beijing   Paris   New York

3. **languages (difficult):**   Russian   Arabic   Chinese

4. **careers (dangerous):**   race car driver   jet pilot   stuntman

Write About Several Schools That You Know

Think Critically About Meaning and Use

A. Complete each conversation.

1. A: Mr. Day's class is the most popular.

B: I know. _____

   a. Nobody likes him.

   (b.) Everyone wants to take it.

   c. Is he shorter than his friends?

2. A: My computer is faster than yours.

B: _____

   a. But is it better?

   b. I know, but mine is the fastest.

   c. Is it slower than mine?

3. A: How hard are diamonds?

B: _____

   a. They're the hardest minerals on earth.

   b. They are the most difficult minerals on earth.

   c. They're harder.

4. A: Why should I take Latin?

B: _____

   a. Because it's the least useful language offered.

   b. Because it's less interesting than Greek.

   c. Because the Latin teacher is the best in the school.

B. Discuss these questions in small groups.

1. EVALUATE In 1, imagine that A says to B, "Mr. Day's class is the least popular." Which choice best completes B's new response?

2. GENERATE In 4, imagine that A asks B, "Should I take Chinese?" B thinks A should, but C thinks A shouldn't. What do they say? (Use superlatives in your answers.)

Edit

Some of these sentences have errors. Find the errors and correct them.

1. Rio is the ~~more~~ *most* exciting city in the world.

2. I'm the worst driver in my family.

3. He's an oldest person in the class.

4. July 28 was the hottest day of the year.

5. This restaurant is not the cheaper one in the city.

6. This is the most slowest bus in this town.

7. She is the smartest than all.

8. They're the carefullest students.

Write

Review exercise C1 on page 393. Write a paragraph comparing and contrasting three schools that you know. Use superlative adjectives and adverbs.

1. **BRAINSTORM** List all the qualities of the schools you are comparing and contrasting. Use these questions to make notes.
   - What is the size of each school?
   - What is the reputation of each school?
   - Where is each school located?
   - Are the dorms comfortable?
   - Are the professors famous?
   - Are the students friendly? Is the campus beautiful?

2. **WRITE A FIRST DRAFT** Before you write your first draft, read the checklist below. Write your draft using superlatives.

3. **EDIT** Read your work and check it against the checklist below. Circle grammar, spelling, and punctuation errors.

DO I ...	YES
form the superlative with one-syllable adjectives and adverbs?	☐
form the superlative with two-syllable adjectives and adverbs?	☐
form the superlative with three-syllable adjectives and adverbs?	☐
include at least two irregular superlatives?	☐
compare three or more things, actions, or people?	☐
make statements of opinion about three or more things?	☐

4. **PEER REVIEW** Work with a partner to help you decide how to fix your errors and improve the content.

5. **REWRITE YOUR DRAFT** Using the comments from your partner, write a final draft.

> My college is better than West College, but Sunrise College is the best college in town. My college has the most students, but Sunrise College has the most famous professors. West College is the oldest...

Choose the correct word or words to complete each sentence.

1. The Pacific Ocean is the biggest ocean _____ all.

   a. than

   b. from

   c. for

   d. of

2. Larry is a good speaker. David speaks _____, too.

   a. well

   b. better

   c. better than

   d. best

3. Today's test was less _____ than last week's test.

   a. difficult

   b. harder

   c. easily

   d. more difficult

4. We go out to eat _____ than you do.

   a. frequently

   b. more frequent

   c. frequent

   d. more frequently

5. Susan types _____ of all the workers.

   a. efficient

   b. efficiently

   c. the most efficiently

   d. more efficiently

6. Sally is _____ than Susan.

   a. friendly

   b. the most friendly

   c. more friendlier

   d. friendlier

Choose the correct response to complete each conversation.

7. **A:** What kinds of books do you like the best?

   B: _____

   a. Science fiction is the least interesting.

   b. Mysteries sell better than biographies.

   c. Novels are my favorites.

   d. Novels are better than mysteries.

8. **A:** Sonia is smarter than everyone in her class.

   B: I disagree. I think _____

   a. Paulo is more popular.

   b. Paulo is the nicest.

   c. Paulo is less smart.

   d. Paulo is the most intelligent.

9. A: My new apartment is the most expensive in the building.

   B: _____

      a. My apartment is new, too.   **c.** It's also the largest.

      b. Why is it cheaper?   **d.** Why is it more expensive?

10. A: Which supermarket has the lowest prices?

   B: _____

      a. Smart Mart is the worst.   **c.** Grocery Depot is the cheapest.

      b. Bentley's has the fewest sales.   **d.** Bentley's is cheaper than Smart Mart.

Match the sentence parts.

11. Ronald Reagan was _____   **a.** the coldest winters.

12. Harvard is _____   **b.** the longest river.

13. Alaska has _____   **c.** the lowest place.

14. California has _____   **d.** the oldest president.

                              e. the oldest college.

                              f. the smallest state.

Complete each sentence with the comparative or superlative form of the word in parentheses.

15. Your directions are _____ (easy) than Jan's.

16. Paul speaks English _____ (well) than his brother.

17. Your cold is _____ (bad) than yesterday.

18. She can run _____ (fast) than I can.

19. Can you type _____ (accurate) than Maria?

20. Monday is _____ (convenient) than Friday for me.

Appendices

1 Spelling of Regular and Irregular Plural Nouns

Regular Plural Nouns

1. For most plural nouns, add -s to the base form.

   apple — apples   lake — lakes
   flower — flowers   river — rivers

2. If the base form ends with the letter *s*, *z*, *sh*, *ch*, or *x*, add -*es*.

   box — boxes   fax — faxes
   bush — bushes   gas — gases

3. If the base form ends with a consonant + *y*, change *y* to *i* and add -*es*. (Compare vowel + *y*: boy — boys; toy — toys.)

   baby — babies
   balcony — balconies
   dictionary — dictionaries

4. If the base form ends with a consonant + *o*, add -*s* or -*es*. Some words take -*s*, some words take -*es*, some take both -*s* and -*es*. (Compare vowel + *o*: radio — radios; zoo — zoos.)

-*s*	-*es*	Both -*s* and -*es*
auto — autos	potato — potatoes	tornado — tornados/tornadoes
photo — photos	tomato — tomatoes	volcano — volcanos/volcanoes
piano — pianos		zero — zeros/zeroes
radio — radios		

5. If the base form of certain nouns ends with a single *f* or in *fe*, change the *f* or *fe* to *v* and add -*es*.

   calf — calves
   shelf — shelves
   knife — knives

Exceptions

belief — beliefs
chief — chiefs
roof — roofs
scarf — scarfs/scarves

Irregular Plural Nouns

child – children	goose – geese	person – people
fish – fish	man – men	tooth – teeth
foot – feet	mouse – mice	woman – women

2 Common Noncount Nouns

Solids	Gases	Materials	Liquids
bread	air	cotton	coffee
butter	carbon dioxide	glass	cream
chalk	oxygen	gold	gasoline
cheese	smoke	iron	juice
chocolate	steam	metal	milk
fish		plastic	oil
meat		silver	rain
pasta		steel	shampoo
rope		wood	soda
soap		wool	soup
			tea
			toothpaste
			water

Grains and Powders	Feelings and Ideas	School Subjects	Activities
cereal	fear	Biology	baseball
detergent	freedom	Economics	basketball
dust	happiness	English	chess
flour	independence	History	football
pepper	information	Mathematics	hiking
rice	knowledge	Physical Education	reading
salt	love	Physics	soccer
sand	sadness	Science	swimming
sugar	time		tennis
wheat	work		

General Categories

candy	furniture
clothing	jewelry
education	luggage
equipment	money
food	weather
fruit	work

3 Spelling of Verbs Ending in *-ing*

1. For most verbs, add *-ing* to the base form of the verb.

   sleep — sleeping   talk — talking

2. If the base form ends in a single *e*, drop the *e* and add *-ing* (exception: be – being).

   live — living   write — writing

3. If the base form ends in *ie*, change *ie* to *y* and add *-ing*.

   die — dying   lie — lying

4. If the base form of a one-syllable verb ends with a single vowel + consonant, double the final consonant and add *-ing*. (Compare two vowels + consonant: eat — eating.)

   hit — hitting   stop — stopping

5. If the base form of a verb with two or more syllables ends in a single vowel + consonant, double the final consonant only if the stress is on the final syllable. Do not double the final consonant if the stress is not on the final syllable.

   admít — admitting   begín — beginning   devélop — developing   lísten — listening

6. Do not double the final consonants *x*, *w*, and *y*.

   fix — fixing   grow — growing   obey — obeying

4 Spelling of Verbs Ending in *-s* and *-es*

1. For most third-person singular verbs, add *-s* to the base form.

   live — lives
   swim — swims

2. If the base form ends with the letter *s*, *z*, *sh*, *ch*, or *x*, add *-es*.

   miss — misses
   teach — teaches

3. If the base form ends with a consonant + *y*, change *y* to *i* and add *-es*.

   study — studies
   try — tries

4. If the base form ends with a consonant + *o*, add *-es*.

   do — does
   go — goes

5 Pronunciation of Verbs and Nouns Ending in -*s* and -*es*

1. If the base form of the verb or noun ends with the sound /s/, /z/, /ʃ/, /ʒ/, /tʃ/, /dʒ/, or /ks/, then pronounce -*es* as an extra syllable /ɪz/.

   Verbs

   slice — slices   watch — watches

   lose — loses   judge — judges

   wash — washes   relax — relaxes

   Nouns

   price — prices   inch — inches

   size — sizes   language — languages

   dish — dishes   tax — taxes

2. If the base form ends with the voiceless sound /p/, /t/, /k/, /f/, or /θ/, then pronounce -*s* and -*es* as /s/.

   Verbs

   sleep — sleeps   work — works

   hit — hits   laugh — laughs

   Nouns

   grape — grapes   book — books

   cat — cats   cuff — cuffs

3. If the base form ends with any other consonant or with a vowel sound, then pronounce -*s* and -*es* as /z/.

   Verbs

   learn — learns

   go — goes

   Nouns

   name — names

   boy — boys

6 Spelling of Verbs Ending in -*ed*

1. To form the simple past of most regular verbs, add -*ed* to the base form.

   brush — brushed   play — played

2. If the base form ends with *e*, just add -*d*.

   close — closed   live — lived

3. If the base form ends with a consonant + *y*, change the *y* to *i* and add -*ed*.
   (Compare vowel +*y*: play — played; enjoy — enjoyed.)

   study — studied   dry — dried

4. If the base form of a one-syllable verb ends with a single vowel + consonant, double the final consonant and add -*ed*.

   plan — planned   shop — shopped

5. If the base form of a verb with two or more syllables ends with a single vowel + consonant, double the final consonant and add -*ed* only when the stress is on the final syllable. Do not double the final consonant if the stress is not on the final syllable.

   prefér — preferred   énter — entered

6. Do not double the final consonants *x*, *w*, and *y*.

   fix — fixed   snow — snowed   stay — stayed

7 Pronunciation of Verbs Ending in -ed

1. If the base form of the verb ends with the sounds /t/ or /d/, then pronounce -ed as an extra syllable /ɪd/.

/t/	/d/
start — started	need — needed
wait — waited	decide — decided

2. If the base form ends with the voiceless sounds /p/, /k/, /f/, /s/, /ʃ/, /tʃ/, or /ks/, then pronounce -ed as /t/.

jump — jumped	laugh — laughed	wish — wished	fax — faxed
look — looked	slice — sliced	watch — watched	

3. If the base form ends with the voiced sounds /b/, /g/, /dʒ/, /m/, /n/, /ŋ/, /l/, /r/, /ð/, /v/, /z/, or with a vowel, then pronounce -ed as /d/.

rob — robbed	hum — hummed	call — called	wave — waved
brag — bragged	rain — rained	order — ordered	close — closed
judge — judged	bang — banged	bathe — bathed	play — played

8 Irregular Verbs

Base Form	Simple Past	Base Form	Simple Past	Base Form	Simple Past
be	was/were	draw	drew	hear	heard
become	became	drink	drank	hide	hid
begin	began	drive	drove	hit	hit
bend	bent	eat	ate	hold	held
bite	bit	fall	fell	hurt	hurt
blow	blew	feed	fed	keep	kept
break	broke	feel	felt	know	knew
bring	brought	fight	fought	lay (= put)	laid
build	built	find	found	lead	led
buy	bought	fly	flew	leave	left
catch	caught	forget	forgot	lend	lent
choose	chose	freeze	froze	let	let
come	came	get	got	lose	lost
cost	cost	give	gave	make	made
cut	cut	go	went	meet	met
dig	dug	grow	grew	pay	paid
dive	dove (OR dived)	hang	hung	put	put
do	did	have	had	quit	quit

Base Form	Simple Past	Base Form	Simple Past	Base Form	Simple Past
read	read	shut	shut	tear	tore
ride	rode	sing	sang	tell	told
ring	rang	sit	sat	think	thought
run	ran	sleep	slept	throw	threw
say	said	speak	spoke	understand	understood
see	saw	spend	spent	wake	woke
sell	sold	steal	stole	wear	wore
send	sent	swim	swam	win	won
shoot	shot	take	took	write	wrote
show	showed	teach	taught		

9 Common Adjectives

Quality/Opinion	Size	Color	Age	Origin	Shape
athletic	big	black	ancient	African	oval
awful	huge	blue	antique	American	rectangular
bright	large	brown	modern	Asian	round
brilliant	little	green	new	Australian	square
cheap	long	gray	old	Brazilian	triangular
cloudy	narrow	orange	old-fashioned	Canadian	
delicious	small	pink	young	Chinese	
expensive	short	purple		European	
famous	tall	red		French	
fantastic	thick	white		German	
handsome	thin	yellow		Indian	
intelligent	tiny			Italian	
interesting	wide			Japanese	
noisy				Korean	
rainy				Latin American	
serious				Middle Eastern	
strong				South American	
terrible				Spanish	
unusual					
useless					
valuable					
wonderful					

10 Adjectives with Two Comparative and Superlative Forms

Adjective	Comparative	Superlative
friendly	friendlier	the friendliest
	more friendly	the most friendly
handsome	handsomer	the handsomest
	more handsome	the most handsome
happy	happier	the happiest
	more happy	the most happy
polite	politer	the politest
	more polite	the most polite
quiet	quieter	the quietest
	more quiet	the most quiet

11 Contractions with Verb and Modal Forms

Contractions with Be

I am	=	I'm
you are	=	you're
he is	=	he's
she is	=	she's
it is	=	it's
we are	=	we're
you are	=	you're
they are	=	they're

I am not	=	I'm not
you are not	=	you're not / you aren't
he is not	=	he's not / he isn't
she is not	=	she's not / she isn't
it is not	=	it's not / it isn't
we are not	=	we're not / we aren't
you are not	=	you're not / you aren't
they are not	=	they're not / they aren't

Contractions with *Will*

I will	=	I'll
you will	=	you'll
he will	=	he'll
she will	=	she'll
it will	=	it'll
we will	=	we'll
you will	=	you'll
they will	=	they'll
will not	=	won't

Contractions with *Was* and *Were*

was not	=	wasn't
were not	=	weren't

Contractions with *Be Going To*

I am going to	=	I'm going to
you are going to	=	you're going to
he is going to	=	he's going to
she is going to	=	she's going to
it is going to	=	it's going to
we are going to	=	we're going to
you are going to	=	you're going to
they are going to	=	they're going to
you are not going to	=	you're not going to / you aren't going to

Contractions with *Do* and *Did*

do not	=	don't
does not	=	doesn't
did not	=	didn't

Contractions with *Can, Could,* and *Should*

cannot	=	can't
could not	=	couldn't
should not	=	shouldn't

12 Answers to Exercises

C3: page 179

		PLACE OF BIRTH	YEAR OF BIRTH
2.	Columbus	Italy	1451 A.D.
3.	Confucius	China	about 551 B.C.
4.	Marie Curie	Poland	1867 A.D.
5.	Einstein	Germany	1879 A.D.
6.	Picasso	Spain	1881 A.D.
7.	Rembrandt	the Netherlands	1606 A.D.
8.	Shakespeare	England	1564 A.D.

C3: page 394

	ANIMALS	WORLD RECORDS
2.	peregrine falcon	This bird can dive at speeds of 270 miles per hour.
3.	anaconda	This snake can grow to a length of 30 feet.
4.	cheetah	This animal can reach a speed of 70 miles per hour.
5.	blue whale	This animal can weigh up to 30 tons.
6.	sea-wasp jellyfish	This sea animal is 30 times more deadly than a cobra.
7.	sea turtle	This sea animal can live to 200 years.
8.	bar-headed goose	This bird can fly above 29,000 feet.

13 Phonetic Symbols

Vowels

i	see /si/	u	too /tu/	oʊ	go /goʊ/
ɪ	sit /sɪt/	ʌ	cup /kʌp/	ɜr	bird /bɜrd/
ɛ	ten /tɛn/	ə	about /əˈbaʊt/	ɪr	near /nɪr/
æ	cat /kæt/	eɪ	say /seɪ/	ɛr	hair /hɛr/
ɑ	hot /hɑt/	aɪ	five /faɪv/	ɑr	car /kɑr/
ɔ	saw /sɔ/	ɔɪ	boy /bɔɪ/	ɔr	north /nɔrθ/
ʊ	put /pʊt/	aʊ	now /naʊ/	ʊr	tour /tʊr/

Consonants

p	pen /pɛn/	f	fall /fɔl/	m	man /mæn/
b	bad /bæd/	v	voice /vɔɪs/	n	no /noʊ/
t	tea /ti/	θ	thin /θɪn/	ŋ	sing /sɪŋ/
t̬	butter /ˈbʌt̬ər/	ð	then /ðɛn/	l	leg /lɛg/
d	did /dɪd/	s	so /soʊ/	r	red /rɛd/
k	cat /kæt/	z	zoo /zu/	j	yes /jɛs/
g	got /gɑt/	ʃ	she /ʃi/	w	wet /wɛt/
tʃ	chin /tʃɪn/	ʒ	vision /ˈvɪʒn/		
dʒ	June /dʒun/	h	how /haʊ/		

Glossary of Grammar Terms

ability modal *See* **modal of ability**.

action Something that you do, usually involving movement, such *as open a door, drink some water, wash your face.*

action verb A verb that describes a thing that someone or something does. An action verb does not describe a state or condition.

> Sam **rang** the bell.
> I **eat** soup for lunch.
> It **rains** a lot here.

activity A lot of action or movement over a period of time, such as *running, dancing, eating, swimming.*

adjective A word that describes or modifies the meaning of a noun.

> the **orange** car
> a **strange** noise

adverb A word that describes or modifies the meaning of a verb, another adverb, an adjective, or a sentence. Many adverbs answer such questions as *How? When? Where?* or *How often?* They often end in -**ly**.

> She ran **quickly**.   She ran **very** quickly.
> a **really** hot day   **Maybe** she'll leave.

adverb of degree An adverb that makes adjectives or other adverbs stronger or weaker.

> She is **extremely** busy this week.
> He performed **very** well during the exam.
> He was **somewhat** surprised by her response.

adverb of frequency An adverb that tells how often a situation occurs. Adverbs of frequency range in meaning from *all of the time to none of the time.*

> She **always** eats breakfast.
> He **never** eats meat.

adverb of manner An adverb that answers the question *How?* and describes the way someone does something or the way something happens. Adverbs of manner usually end in -**ly**.

> He walked **slowly**.
> It rained **heavily** all night.

adverb of opinion An adverb that expresses an opinion about an entire sentence or idea.

> **Luckily**, we missed the traffic.
> **We** couldn't find a seat on the train, **unfortunately**.

adverb of time An adverb that answers the question *When?* and refers to either a specific time or a more indefinite time.

> Let's leave **tonight** instead of **tomorrow**.
> They **recently** opened a new store.

adverbial phrase A phrase that functions as an adverb.

> Amy spoke **very softly**.

affirmative statement A sentence that does not have a negative verb.

> Linda went to the movies.

agree To have a grammatical relationship with. In English subjects and verbs agree in person and number, for example, *I am..., You are..., He is...*

agreement The subject and verb of a clause must agree in number. If the subject is singular, the verb form is also singular. If the subject is plural, the verb form is also plural.

> **He comes** home early.
> **They come** home early.

article The words **a**, **an**, and **the** in English. Articles are used to introduce and identify nouns.

> **a** potato   **an** onion   **the** supermarket

auxiliary verb A verb that is used before main verbs (or other auxiliary verbs) in a sentence. Auxiliary verbs are usually used in questions and negative sentences. **Do**, **have**, and **be** can act as auxiliary verbs. Modals (**may**, **can**, **will**, and so on) are also auxiliary verbs.

> **Do** you have the time?
> I **have** never been to Italy.
> The car **was** speeding.
> I **may** be late.

base form The form of a verb without any verb endings; the infinitive form without *to*. Also called *simple form*.

> sleep   be   stop

clause A group of words that has a subject and a verb. *See also* **dependent clause** and **main clause**.

> If I leave,…
> The rain stopped.
> …when he speaks.
> …that I saw.

common noun A noun that refers to any of a class of people, animals, places, things, or ideas. Common nouns are not capitalized.

> man   cat   city   pencil   grammar

comparative A form of an adjective, adverb, or noun that is used to express differences between two items or situations.

> This book is **heavier than** that one.
> He runs **more quickly than** his brother.
> A CD costs **more money than** a cassette.

consonant A speech sound that is made by partly or completely stopping the air as it comes out of the mouth. For example, with the sounds /p/, /d/, and /g/, the air is completely stopped. With the sounds /s/, /f/, and /l/, the air is partly stopped.

contraction The combination of two words into one by omitting certain letters and replacing them with an apostrophe.

> I will = **I'll** we are = **we're** are not = **aren't**

count noun A common noun that you can count as an individual thing. It usually has both a singular and a plural form.

> orange — oranges   woman — women

definite article The word **the** in English. It is used to identify nouns based on information the speaker and listener share about the noun. The definite article is also used for making general statements about a whole class or group of nouns.

> Please give me **the** key.
> **The** scorpion is dangerous.

demonstrative adjective **This**, **that**, **these**, and **those** are demonstrative adjectives when they occur before nouns. They tell whether the noun is near or far from the speaker.

> **This** house is nice. **That** house isn't.
> **These** books are due at the library. **Those** books aren't.

demonstrative pronoun **This**, **that**, **these**, and **those** are demonstrative pronouns when they take the place of a demonstrative adjective + noun.

> **This** is new. (This book is new.)
> **That** is old. (That book is old.)
> **These** are ready. (These cookies are ready.)
> **Those** aren't ready. (Those cookies aren't ready.)

dependent clause A clause that cannot stand alone as a sentence because it depends on the main clause to complete the meaning of the sentence. Also called *subordinate clause*.

> I'm going home **after he calls**.

determiner A word such as **a**, **an**, **the**, **this**, **that**, **these**, **those**, **my**, **some**, **a few**, and **three** that is used before a noun to limit its meaning in some way.

> **those** videos

direct object A noun or pronoun that refers to a person or thing that is directly affected by the action of a verb.

> John wrote **a letter**.
> Please buy **some milk**.

first person One of the three classes of personal pronouns. First person refers to the person (*I*) or people (*we*) who are actually speaking or writing.

formal A style of speech or writing where the speaker or writer is very careful about pronunciation, choice of words, and sentence structure. Formal language is used at official functions, ceremonies, speeches, in the law and in other types of serious writing.

> "Ladies and Gentlemen, allow me to introduce a man to whom I owe a great deal of gratitude…"

future A time that is to come. The future is expressed in English with **will**, **be going to**, the simple present, or the present continuous. These different forms of the future often have different meanings and uses.

> I **will** help you later.
> David **is going to** call later.
> The train **leaves** at 6:05 this evening.
> I'm **driving** to Toronto tomorrow.

general quantity expression A quantity expression that indicates whether a quantity or an amount is large or small. It does not give an exact amount.

> **a lot of** cookies   **a little** flour
> **a few** people   **some** milk

general statement A generalization about a whole class or group of nouns.

> Whales are mammals.
> A daffodil is a flower that grows from a bulb.

gerund An -**ing** form of a verb that is used in place of a noun or pronoun to name an activity or a state.

> **Skiing** is fun.   He doesn't like **being sick**.

imperative A type of sentence, usually without a subject, that tells someone to do something. The verb is in the base form.

> **Open** your books to page 36.
> **Be** ready at eight.

impersonal *you* The use of the pronoun you to refer to people in general rather than a particular person or group of people.

> Nowadays **you** can buy anything on the Internet.

indefinite article The words **a** and **an** in English. Indefinite articles introduce a noun as a member of a class of nouns or make generalizations about a whole class or group of nouns.

> Please hand me **a** pencil.
> **An** ocean is **a** large body of water.

independent clause *See* **main clause**.

indirect object A noun or pronoun used after some verbs that refers to the person who receives the direct object of a sentence.

> John wrote a letter **to Mary**.
> Please buy some milk **for us**.

infinitive A verb form that includes **to** + the base form of a verb. An infinitive is used in place of a noun or pronoun to name an activity or state expressed by a verb.

> Do you like **to swim**?

informal A style of speech, and sometimes writing, used in everyday conversations between friends, co-workers, and family members. In informal speech, the speaker is casual about pronunciation, choice of words, and sentence structure. Informal speech is often fast speech with a lot of reduced and contracted forms. Short notes, email messages, and written dialogues are often informal.

information question A question that begins with a **wh**- word.

> Where does she live?
> Who lives here?

intonation The change in pitch, loudness, syllable length, and rhythm in spoken language.

intransitive verb A verb that cannot be followed by an object.

> We finally **arrived**.

irregular verb A verb that does not form the simple past by adding -*d* or -*ed* endings.

> put — put
> buy — bought

main clause A clause that can be used by itself as a sentence. Also called *independent clause*.

> I'm going home.

main verb A verb that can be used alone in a sentence. A main verb can also occur with an auxiliary verb.

> I **ate** lunch at 11:30.
> Kate can't **eat** lunch today.

modal The auxiliary verbs **can**, **could**, **may**, **might**, **must**, **should**, **will**, and **would**. They modify the meaning of a main verb by expressing ability, authority, formality, politeness, or various degrees of certainty. Also called *modal auxiliary*.

> You **should** take something for your headache.
> Applicants **must** have a high school diploma.

modal of ability Can and could are called modals of ability when they express the ability to do something.

> He **can** speak Arabic and English.
> **Can** you play the piano?
> Yesterday we **couldn't** leave during the storm.
> Seat belts **can** save lives.

modal of permission May, could, and can are called modals of permission when they are used to ask for, give, or refuse permission to do something.

> A: **May** I leave early?
> B: Yes, you **can**.
> A: Mom, **could** I stay up late tonight?
> B: No, you **may not**. You have school tomorrow.

modal auxiliary *See* **modal**.

modify To add to or change the meaning of a word.

> Adjectives modify nouns (**expensive** cars).
> Adverbs modify verbs (**very** fast).

negative statement A sentence with a negative verb.

> I **didn't see** that movie.
> He **isn't** happy.

non-action verb *See* **stative verb**.

noncount noun A common noun that cannot be counted. A noncount noun has no plural form and cannot occur with **a**, **an**, or a number.

> information   mathematics   weather

noun A word that typically refers to a person, animal, place, thing, or idea.

> Tom   rabbit   store   computer
> mathematics

noun phrase A phrase formed by a noun and its modifiers. A noun phrase can substitute for a noun in a sentence.

> She drank **milk**.
> She drank **chocolate milk**.
> She drank **the milk**.

object A noun, pronoun, or noun phrase that follows a transitive verb or a preposition.

> He likes **pizza**.
> She likes **him**.
> Go with **her**.
> Steve threw **the ball**.

object pronoun The pronouns **me**, **you** (sg., pl.), **him**, **her**, **it**, **us**, and **them** are object pronouns when they act as the object of a verb or preposition.

past continuous A verb form that expresses an activity in progress at a specific time in the past. The past continuous is formed with **was** or **were** + verb + **-ing**. Also called *past progressive*.

> A: What **were** you **doing** last night at eight o'clock?
> B: I **was studying**.

past progressive *See* **past continuous**.

phrasal modal A verb that is not a true modal, but has the same meaning as a modal verb. Examples of phrasal modals are **ought to**, **have to**, and **have got to**.

phrase A group of words that can form a grammatical unit. A phrase can take the form of a noun phrase, verb phrase, adjective phrase, adverbial phrase, or prepositional phrase. This means it can act as a noun, verb, adjective, adverb, or preposition.

> The **tall man** left.
> Lee **hit the ball**.
> The child was **very quiet**.
> She spoke **too fast**.
> They ran **down the stairs**.

plural The form of a word that refers to more than one person or thing. For example, **cats** and **children** are the plural forms of **cat** and **child**.

preposition A word such as **at, in, on,** or **to,** that links nouns, pronouns, and gerunds to other words.

prepositional phrase A phrase that consists of a preposition followed by a noun or noun phrase.

   on Sunday   under the table

present continuous A verb form that indicates that an activity is in progress, temporary, or changing. It is formed with **be** + verb + **-ing.**
Also called *present progressive.*

   I'm **watering** the garden.
   Ruth **is working** for her uncle.
   He**'s getting** better.

present progressive *See* **present continuous.**

pronoun A word that can replace a noun or noun phrase. **I, you, he, she, it, mine,** and **yours** are some examples of pronouns.

proper noun A noun that is the name of a particular person, animal, place, thing, or idea. Proper nouns begin with capital letters and are usually not preceded by **the.**

   Peter   Rover   India   Apollo 13   Buddhism

quantity expression A word or words that occur before a noun to express a quantity or amount of that noun.

   a lot of rain
   few books
   four trucks

reduced form A shortened form of a word or phrase that is common in fast, informal speech.

   "Need any help?" (Do you need any help?)
   "I'm gonna call you." (I'm going to call you.)

regular verb A verb that forms the simple past by adding **-ed, -d,** or changing **y** to **i** and then adding **-ed** to the simple form.

   hunt — hunted
   love — loved
   cry — cried

response An answer to a question, or a reply to other types of spoken or written language.

   A: Are you hungry?
   B: **Yes, in fact I am. Let's eat.**

second person One of the three classes of personal pronouns. Second person refers to the person (**you,** singular) or people (**you,** plural) who are the listeners or readers.

short answer An answer to a *Yes/No* question that has yes or no plus the subject and an auxiliary verb.

   A: Do you speak Chinese?
   B: **Yes, I do. / No, I don't.**

simple form *See* **base form.**

simple past A verb tense that expresses actions and situations that were completed at a definite time in the past.

   Carol **ate** lunch.
   She **was** hungry.

simple present A verb tense that expresses general statements, especially about habitual or repeated activities and permanent situations.

   Every morning I **catch** the 8:00 bus.
   The earth **is** round.

singular The form of a word that refers to only one person or thing. For example, **cat** and **child** are the singular forms of **cats** and **children.**

standard form A form of language that is based on the speech and writing of educated native speakers of a language. Standard language is used in the news media and other public speech, in literature, in textbooks, and other academic materials. It is described in dictionaries and grammar books.

state Physical conditions, senses, possession, knowledge, feelings, and measurements are states that are expressed with be and other non-action (stative) verbs.

   She **is tall.**
   The flower **smells good.**
   He **owns a house.**

stative verb A type of verb that is not usually used in the continuous form because it expresses a condition or state that is not changing. **Know, love, resemble, see,** and **smell** are some examples. Also called *non-action verb*.

stress The pronunciation of a syllable or word with more force than the pronunciation of surrounding syllables or words. Stressed syllables or words often sound louder and longer than surrounding syllables or words.

> I didn't see **Susan,** I saw **John.**

subject A noun, pronoun, or noun phrase that precedes the verb phrase in a sentence. The subject of a sentence with be tells who or what the sentence is about. The subject of a sentence with an action verb tells who did or caused the action.

> **The park** is huge.
> **Erica** kicked the ball.

subject pronoun The pronouns **I, you** (sg., pl.), **he, she, it, we,** and **they** are subject pronouns when they act as the subject of a clause.

subordinate clause *See* **dependent clause.**

superlative A form of an adjective, adverb, or noun used to compare a group of three or more people, things, or actions. The superlative shows that one member of the group has more (or less) than all of the others.

> This perfume has **the strongest** scent.
> He speaks **the fastest** of all.
> That machine makes **the most noise** of the three.

syllable A word or part of a word that contains one vowel sound.

> **Happy** has two syllables: **hap-py**
> **Dictionary** has four syllables: **dic-tion-ar-y**

tense The form of a verb that shows past, present, and future time.

> He **lives** in New York now.
> He **lived** in Washington two years ago.
> He'll **live** in Toronto next year.

third person One of the three classes of personal pronouns. Third person refers to some person (**he, she**), people (**they**), or thing (**it**) other than the speaker/writer or listener/reader.

time expression A phrase that functions as an adverb of time.

> She graduated **three years ago.**
> I'll see them **the day after tomorrow.**

transitive verb A verb that is followed by an object.

> I **read** the book.

verb A word that refers to an action or a state.

> Gina **closed** the window.
> Tim **loves** classical music.

verb phrase A phrase that has a main verb and any objects, adverbs, or dependent clauses that complete the meaning of the verb in the sentence.

> She is **talking.**
> Who **called you?**
> He **walked slowly.**

voiced Refers to speech sounds that are made by vibrating the vocal cords. Examples of voiced sounds are /b/, /d/, and /g/.

> bat   dot   get

voiceless Refers to speech sounds that are made without vibrating the vocal cords. Examples of voiceless sounds are /p/, /t/, and /f/.

> up   it   if

vowel A speech sound that is made with the lips and teeth open. The air from the lungs is not blocked at all. For example, the sounds /a/, /o/, and /i/ are vowels.

wh- word Who, whom, what, where, when, why, how, and which are wh- words. They are used to ask questions and to connect clauses.

Yes/No question A question that can be answered with the words **yes** or **no.**

> Can you drive a car?
> Does he live here?

Index

This Index is for the full and split editions. Entries for Volume B are in bold.

A

a/an, *see also* Indefinite articles and adjectives, 90–91, **223**
meaning and use of, 226
and plural count nouns, 65, 77
with singular count nouns, 62–63, 76, **222**, **223**
with *there is/there are*, **251**
Ability, with *can* and *could*
forms of, 308–310
meaning and use of, 312
Actions, *see* Action verbs
Action verbs, 4
Activities, *see also* Conditions; Events in sequence; Simultaneous activities; Situations; States
activities in progress
and past continuous, 210
and present continuous, 127
and infinitives and gerunds, 366
noncount nouns for, 80
and simple past, 197, 210
Adjectives, *see also* Descriptive adjectives
and articles, 223
comparatives of
forms of, 376–377
meaning and use of, 380
demonstrative adjectives, 111–112
possessive adjectives
forms of, 103
meaning and use of, 106
and possessive pronouns, 108
superlatives of
forms of, 388–390
meaning and use of, 392

Adverbs
comparatives of
forms of, 376–377
meaning and use of, 380
superlatives of
forms of, 388–389
meaning and use of, 392
there, **256**
Adverbs of frequency, 153–166
forms of, 156–157
meaning and use of, 160–161
Advice, with *should*, 338
a few, **234**, **235**, **240**, **241**
Affirmative short answers, *see* **Short answers**
Affirmative statements, *see* **Statements**
after that, 149
Age
adjectives for, 93
descriptions of, with *be*, 21
ago, 178
Agreeing to requests, 324, 325
a little, **234**, **235**, **240**, **241**
all the time, 160
almost always, 157, 160, 161
almost never, 157, 160, 161
a lot, **235**
a lot of, **234**, **235**, **240**, **241**
always, 156, 157, 160, 161
am, see *be*
am not, 18
and
with adjectives, 90
combining sentences with, 130
vs. *while*, 211
any, **234**, **235**, **251**
Apostrophe
in contractions, 13
for possessive nouns, 102
are/aren't, see *be*

are not, 18
Articles, 219–230, *see also* Definite articles; Indefinite articles; No article
meaning and use of, 226–227
Asking for permission, 325
at the moment, 127
Auxiliary verbs, with comparatives, 377

B

Base form of verb
with *be going to*, 268–269
with *can* and *could*, 308–309
in imperatives, 46
with *may* and *might*, 296–297
with modals of request and permission, 320–321
and past continuous, 206–207
and present continuous, 122–123
with *should* and *must*, 334–335
in simple past, 186–187, 192–193
in simple present, 136, 137, 140
with *will* (for future), 282–283
be, 8–56, **see also *be going to*; *there is/there are***
adjectives after, 90
with comparatives, 377
contractions with
in affirmative statements, 13
with *be going to*, 268–269
it's, 103
in negative statements, 18
noun + *is*, 103
in short answers, 31
of subject pronouns, 13, 122–123

Grammar Sense

ONLINE PRACTICE

How to Register for Grammar Sense Online Practice

Follow the steps to register for *Grammar Sense Online Practice*.

1. Go to www.grammarsensepractice.com and click on **Register**

2. Read and agree to the terms of use. **I Agree.**

3. Enter the Access Code that came with your Student Book. Your code is written on the inside back cover of your book.

   ☐ ☐ ☐ ☐ **Enter**

4. Enter your personal information (first and last name, email address, and password).

5. Click on the Student Book that you are using for your class.

   > It is very important to select your book. You are using Grammar Sense 1. Please click the **GREEN** Grammar Sense 1 cover.

   If you don't know which book to select, **STOP**. Continue when you know your book.

6. Enter your class ID to join your class, and click NEXT. Your class ID is on the line below, or your teacher will give it to you on a different piece of paper.

   _____ **Next**

   You don't need a class ID code. If you do not have a class ID code, click Skip. To enter this code later, choose Join a Class from your Home page.

7. Once you're done, click on Enter Online Practice to begin using *Grammar Sense Online Practice*.

   Enter Online Practice

Next time you want to use *Grammar Sense Online Practice*, just go to www.grammarsensepractice.com and log in with your email address and password.